DIMENSIONS OF SOCIAL ISSUES IN INDIA'S NORTH-EAST

Selections on Youth, Drugs, Education and Unemployment

DIMENSIONS OF SOCIAL ISSUES IN INDIA'S NORTH-EAST

Selections on Youth, Drugs, Education and Unemployment

Edited by

H. Sudhir

Jubita Hajarimayum

AKANSHA PUBLISHING HOUSE

NEW DELHI-110002 (INDIA)

AKANSHA PUBLISHING HOUSE
4649-B/21, Ansari Road
Darya Ganj, New Delhi - 110 002
Ph.: 23263193/9811582579
Fax: 011-23263193
Email: ektabooks@yahoo.com

Dimensions of Social Issues in India's North-east: Selections on Youth, Drugs, Education and Unemployment

First Published 2007

ISBN–978–81–8370–113-6

[The responsibility for the facts stated, conclusions reached etc., is entirely that of the authors/editors. The publisher is not responsible for them, whatsoever.]

PRINTED IN INDIA

Published by **M.P. Misra** for **Akansha Publishing House**, New Delhi and Printed at Aryan Enterprises, Delhi.

PREFACE

The present volume has originated from a seminar and a workshop organized by the Ereima Gender Empowerment and Resource Centre (EGERC), Imphal, Manipur under the auspices of the Indian Council of Social Science Research (ICSSR), New Delhi held at Imphal, on 20-21 February 2003 and 24-25 June 2004 respectively. The programmes were conceptualized as a part of the larger initiative to evolve joint partnership for different sectors to understand meaningfully these problems which closely adhesive with the youth, the vulnerable target social group and also to enhance culturally contextual approach towards responding the issues pragmatically.

Sensing the serious urgency of the problems, the programmes purposely provided conducive spaces to a host of potential personalities with a sole goal of synthesizing research findings and field wisdom and towards evolving enabling collaborative initiative to challenge these social issues successfully for a new era of progress.

We feel that this anthology of selected papers, which have emerged from the programmes, would be a piecemeal contribution in the way of appraising these phenomena that poise a threat in this region.

H. SUDHIR
JUBITA HAJARIMAYUM

ACKNOWLEDGEMENTS

We are grateful to the Indian Council of Social Science Research (ICSSR), New Delhi for financial grants, which enabled the programmes to be successfully organized. EGERC research team of Bhavina Sharma, Nirjalata, Lakhikanta, Joyshri deserve appreciation for their efforts towards making the present work to arrive at this final shape.

Thanks are due to H. Suresh for editorial assistance and also to S. Bimol for technical support.

A word of special thanks is to M.P. Misra, Akansha Publishing House, New Delhi for his kind co-operation and publishing this work.

H. SUDHIR
JUBITA HAJARIMAYUM

CONTENTS

Preface v

Acknowledgements vii

List of Tables xi

List of Contributors xiii

1. Introduction 1

2. Relationship between the drug related personal characteristic of addict and socio-cultural and economic factors 10
   —S. Romeobala Devi

3. KABP Studies on Safer Practices of Injecting Drug Among the **IDUs**, Manipur 20
   —K. Ingocha Singh

4. Gender Relation and its Health Implication Among Women: Manipur Case 24
   —Jubita Hajarimayum

5. Drug Use and the Need for Social Advocacy Among Adolescents 34
   —Salam Irene

6. A Perspective on Drug Abuse amongst Youths in Manipur 50
   —Chitra Ahanthem

7. Drug-Abuse: Issues for Development 56
   —E. Bijoy Kumar Singh

8. Youth, Drug and Development: Spading Linkages - 64
—H. Sudhir

9. Opium and Heroin Production in Myanmar and its Impact in the Neighbouring Countries 76
—L. Suresh

10. Unemployment in Manipur: Some policy Implications 89
—Gurudas Das & K. Gyanendra Singh

11. Entrepreneurship Education and Training: It's Role in Solving Unemployment Problems in Manipur 98
—G.P. Prasain

12. Employment opportunities in North East India 111
—Indraneel Bhowmik

13. Youth unrest in Mnaipur 128
—Pradip Phanjoubam

Appendix
Some Parameters of Development in North-east 139

Bibliography 141

Index 146

LIST OF TABLES

8.1	Age-sex proportion of HIV positive cases (Sero-Surveillance)	67
8.2	HIV/AIDS Sero-Sentinel Surveillance – Manipur	68
8.3	District-wise break-up of HIV Positive Cases – Manipur	69
8.4	Sero-posivity and percentage of the intravenous drug users out of total HIV positives – Manipur	69
8.5	Sero-Surveillance	70
10.1	Employment exchange statistics – State-wise 1997	90
10.2	Registration and placing done through employment exchanges in Manipur	92
10.3	Revised net state domestic product of Manipur at constant 1980-81 prices by industry of origin	94
10.4	Distribution of working population by industry	95
12.1	Sectoral Composition of the NE States 2000-01	113
12.2	Progress of Agriculture: Yield of food grains in NE	114
12.3	Land Utilization in North East Region (1995-96)	115
12.4	Number of unemployed registered with the employment exchange of the Government of Tripura	118
12.5	Additional employment created	119
12.6	Employment elasticity of different sectors	120
12.7	Growth rate of employment	126

LIST OF CONTRIBUTORS

Ahanthem, Chitra, North-East India Harm Reduction Network, NEIHRN

Bhowmik, Indraneel, Assistant Professor, Department of Economics, Ambedkar College, Tripura

Devi, S. Romeobala, Counsellor In-Charge, Imphal West District Police Headquarters, Imphal

Das, Gurudas, Reader, & Head Deptt. of Humanities and Social Science, NIT-Silchar, Assam

Hajarimayum, Jubita, Secretary, EGERC, Imphal

Irene, Salam, Associate Professor, Department of History, Manipur University, Manipur

Prasain, G.P., Associate Professor, Department of Commerce, Manipur University

Phanjoubam, Pradip, Editor, Imphal Free Press, Manipur

Singh, K. Ingocha, Community Worker, Lifeline Foundation, Imphal

Singh, E. BijoyKumar, Professor, Department of Economics, Manipur University, Manipur

Sudhir, H., Assistant Professor, Department of History Manipur University, Manipur

Suresh, L., Medical Officer, PRDA

Singh, K. Gyanendra, Research Scholar Department of Economics, NEHU, Shillong

1

INTRODUCTION

—H. Sudhir
—Jubita Hajarimayum

Beginnings

Drug abuse particularly among the youth, which has a deep reaching impact in the larger context of social security and development, is recognized as a serious social concern. Since olden days, the history of mankind has an account of drug usages. Record shows herbs, roots, leaves and plants having used for medical purposes, however, over the past few years, use of drugs against medical meaning has shaken the globe that influenced the world community to respond to the issue.

Drug abuse is an increasing phenomenon in South and South-east Asia. Asian countries clearly demonstrated this phenomenon in the 1980s and the trend continued throughout. The northeast region nestled proximately on the Golden Triangle, which is famous for 20% of world heroin contribution precisely for production of pure heroin type crystal white injectable powder locally known as No.4. Geo-politically, the region has perforated international boundaries. From being a route in the lucrative drug trafficking, the region became a transit-consumer region characterized by an emergent youth's drug addictive behaviour at a large proportion by the 80s and its consequential impact in the society. The youth's addictive behaviour in the region has been largely influenced by a ray complex factors that include inadequate education; want for social support system including youth counselling and health facilities; high scale of unemployment; lack of recreational spaces; usual confrontation to violence; broken familial background; inappropriate parental care; frustration; easier availability of heroin etc.

A serious concern closely associated with the drug addictive behaviour is the endemic called HIV/AIDS. Against the homosexual origin of the epidemic in the United States, the historical genesis of the endemic in this region is related to the high risk addictive behaviour among the injecting drug users transmitted in its own multiplied ways. A considerable percentage of drug users and HIV infected population is in the age group of 15-35 years. The dimension of the issue of drug abuse and HIV/AIDS is serious because it is beyond an individual matter rather a social issue. The more complexity of the issue is its concealed built-up character, costly intervention and programme implementation.

Along with drug addiction, there are questions on education and unemployment, which characterized the region. With the spread of education, the critical situation of unemployment more specifically among the educated youth and its social consequence has been a unique character in this region since the last few years. In spite of raising the number of educational institutions, higher enrolment rate of students to various educational institutions generating to a gradually raising literacy rate, a sizeable chunk of educated youth produced in and out of the state are deprived of remunerative work. This issue of the region is adhesive to its characteristics such as economic backwardness, infrastructural devoid, uneven regional development patterns, absence of medium and large scale industries, dying of public sector industrial ventures, want for of effective incentive to small scale and household industries. On the one side, the government's various self-employment and income generation schemes primarily meant for the educated unemployed need to be made more effective towards realizing meaningfully the desired expectation.

While unemployment is recognized as a situation where one is capable to work yet, unable to find it. It is an involuntary failure to get hold of income generating work. On the economic framework, the issue of educated unemployment is largely determined by the supply-demand relation. The phenomenal expansion of 'supply side' in terms of high population growth rate, expansion of educational institutions and considerate amount of educated youth brought forth both in and out the state is unproportionately commensurated by the 'demand factors' like the sluggish development trend, least employment absorption potentials, educated youths' white collar 'job seeking attitude rather than job providing aptitude' and so forth. The current type of education in the region needs to be given an accord. The region shows a trend of general education with least emphasis on professional and technical education. There is a need for a co-relation between the education system and employment in the region. The present education system requires attuning to the changing development scenario.

Of the total official unemployment data, the educated unemployment shares the lion's share. Apart from the official data, there is a mass of educated unemployeds unregistered in the employment exchanges. Though the number of educated unemployment shows a real concern year by year, the actual placement done is comparatively quite low indicating an employment registration-placement imbalance. This acute problem has been worsened by the ban on fresh recruitments in the government sector.

Of the problems confronted by the educated youth, unemployment is a serious one for the simple reason that it is much more beyond an isolated issue of the educated youth themselves rather an overall social issue. The problem besides affecting the individual educated unemployed and his familial set-up, it too affects the larger social fiber. At the individual point, the unemployment wrecks the identity, psychology and status of an educated youth but also failure on his part to fulfill the due familial expectation disturbs the familial cordial relation at the family level. At the larger social context, a great mass of educated unemployment perpetrating in the society unsolved is a great loss of the most vibrant social group unchanneled in the state's productivity. The serious danger of this continued problem is the liability of the youth to the prey of deviant behaviour, which might be detrimental to the region's overall development. The social and political tranquility of the state and the nation as whole is squarely related to the youth who remained unemployment. The overall development of the country is largely depended on the viable and cultural specific planning and policies that may alleviate the problem.

Unemployment among the uneducated youth is now a subject-matter of considerable debate for the policy-makers, administrators and academicians. The meaningful alleviation of the problem needs to be looked from a wholistic perspective. Despite Government's initiatives to response effectively to the problem in the forms of various employment schemes for the educated youth under the overall development process, there are still inconsistencies in functioning or implementation of the programmes towards adequately benefiting the target group thereby necessarily calling forth an integrated alternative strategy specified to the problem. The need for an appropriate institutional framework to implement educated unemployment alleviation programme touching several aspects viz, state, non-government organization, educated youth, academic and community participation is felt to ensure maximum efficiency. The need is to encourage an integrated participatory approach in planning, implementing, and managing feasible productive employment policies linked to the specific regional infrastructural requirements.

Broad Objective

Taking a serious note of the escalated problem, the current work intends to step in into the task that aims to understand the crux of the problem and also aims to explore and develop the viable cultural and gender specific integrated strategies on collaborative partnership of the different professional expertises to respond effectively to the problem and to enhance effective intervention to alleviate the problem towards region's development orientation. Broadly the work touched upon the extent; dynamics of the problem; overall impact of the problem at different levels at individual, family and social levels; social attitude that causes barriers to the educated youth seeking employment; national and state response; relation of the problems with the region's development status; gap between the policy planning of the government and its implementation part; inter-relation between the various schemes envisaged in the government policy and the actual problem; suggested strategies towards effectively responding the problem.

Précis of the Canvas

Dr. Romeobala begins the analysis conceding the escalating trend of drug abuse among the youth and its impact on the individual addicts and larger social implications. The easier accessibility of drugs in the region has been undoubtedly caused by its nearness to the golden triangle from where drugs are being trafficked to four identified main drug routes and many unidentified forest tracks. Different types of drugs either 'soft and hard drugs' or narcotic and non-narcotic, which have different side effects, are discussed. The core of the analysis lies in the examination of the relationship between the personal characteristics of the drug addicts and socio-cultural and economic factors. The analysis is made on three sets of variables as parameters viz., education, occupation and income. The author feels the need to combat the problem on both curative and preventive approaches and also to save the youth from the clutch of the menace.

In his paper, Ingocha makes an endeavour to explore Knowledge Attitude Behaviour Practices on safer practices among the IDUs based on field survey conducted within the Imphal Municipal Council to evaluate the mid term achievement of the intervention project. The aim of the paper is to understand the IDUS regarding concept and knowledge on safer injecting practices; perception and belief on the safer injecting practices and practice of injecting drugs. The findings show that the majority of IDUs within the 20-29 age category who are mostly literate with a highest number in the higher secondary level. Numerical data show that the majority of the IDUs are from joint familial backgrounds, unmarried and unemployed though a small number in the government salaried jobs. Besides, the data contain many more field information to understand this vulnerable social group of IDUs.

Jubita tries to explore the inter-connectivity between the question of women's health status focusing on STI including HIV and gender relations. Based on the field study, the paper shares the ramifications of gender differentials on women's health like their low socio-economic status, sexual and reproductive vulnerability, gender based violence, less health education and health facility etc. The paper highlights the increasing rate of HIV among the women and children as indicative of lower status, less autonomy, less decision making power and lack of health rights. The paper feels a specific need for women's health movement. In addition to valuing the traditional culture that supports women's higher autonomy, the paper gives a thought on modern universal standards that promote gender oriented development.

To begin, Dr Irene offers illegal drug production that has undergone globalization in the past few decades, co-ordinated distribution network of drugs and witnessing of the drug phenomenon in the northeast region in the 80's. The paper stresses the porous Indo-Myanmar border, lack of vigilance and 'trans border ethnic congruity' leading to drug flow from the golden triangle or more drug refineries to the northeast region. The author argues the prevailing drug policies, which she feels, hard and paradoxical in its enforcement. She discuses addictive behaviour among the youth IDUs, its HIV/AIDS linkage and social implications. She feels the imperative for a strong social advocacy among the adolescents that could effectively challenge the issue of drug addiction among the adolescents.

Chitra's paper touches three factors, which have contributed in making the drug abuse as a serious issue in the world today. The paper is about inter-linkages of drug abuse with its consequential implications on health, economy and society. The author talks about compelling reasons that have dragged the youth to drug addictive behaviour and also provides proposed suggestions in a way to understand the issue.

Though studies on the linkages between drugs or HIV/AIDS and development issue have already made in the areas like Sub-Saharan, the area remains still new in the region. Here, two papers, one by Dr. Bijoy and another by Sudhir are exercises, which try to see the issue. Dr Bijoy argues the dynamics of interactional linkages between drug abuse and development question in a backward sub national economy of the region. An economist's perception is reflected in the analysis of drug abuse and its multifaceted ramifications on the larger development issue. The author writes that drug abuse and its associated impact adversely affect the parameters of economic growth and also income distribution. The impact of drug abuse on development has been examined in terms of labour and capital on growth model. The paper examines the two-way relationship where drug abuse adversely affects development and the lack of development making youth to drug. The author feels a need to check the current pace of this phenomenon in the region otherwise an adverse impact on development index.

The paper by Sudhir is an attempt that tries to dig up the linkages between the drug abuse and development question. He analyses inherent social forces that have pushed the youth to drug addictive behaviour, geo-politics that fosters the drug environ and its social development linkage in the region. The author feels the necessity of maintaining what he describes as social security of the youth from the drug menace for a bright future. He appeals a pragmatic, holistic and culturally contextual appropriate response on collaborative partnership in trying to understand the issue.

Dr Suresh argues about opium, heroin or morphine production in Myanmar and its impact in neighboring countries. Discussion shows a brief history of opium, problem of drug scenario in the state of Manipur and its overall effect on socio- economic and demographic profile.

In this combined initiative, the authors Gurudas Das and Gyanendra supply an analysis of the sectoral character of economy of the state of Manipur. Talking about the linkage of the educated youth and unemployment problem, authors feel a need to focus on the secondary sector. Nonetheless, a stress is made on organic inter-relations among sectors of economy for a mutual growth. Given the situation of the state, there is a need for public sector to play a major role in gearing up the secondary sector but on a suggestive alternative model in collaboration with CBO rather than through the bureaucratic steel frame.

G.P. Prasain's paper for convenient reading can be broadly divided into two parts. While the first part provides a glimpse of national level unemployment scene, the second section devotes the issue in the state of Manipur. The core of the discussion is the need for introducing entrepreneurship education and training in educational institutions e.g., colleges and university as an effective initiative towards responding the issue. The author is of the view that development of entrepreneurship would contribute the generation of employment opportunities and in reducing the issue particularly among the educated youth.

This paper by Indraneel Bhowmick looks at the development perspective from the economic point of view. It attempts to identify the problems faced by youths of the region and further tries to suggest remedies at both micro and macro level. The study utilizes secondary data from different sources and the methodology adopted includes standard econometric application through standard statistical tools.

The character of the youth unrest in the northeast region including Manipur in his paper by Pradeep Phanjoubam is linked up with the totality of breaking established order. The paper sees government's fiscal mess, breaking law and order, institutionalized corruption, becoming of politics as a game of defection and floor crossing, beaurocracy becoming kleptocracy, lack of merit criteria as indicative of the order against which the binding treads of the social fabric too weakened. The issue of the youth is assessed against this background.

At the moment, the brightest hope for a shift in the present geopolitics to lift the northeast out of the current blind spot of the world is a political and economic ferment in neighbouring Myanmar. Our location then, as a bridgehead between the huge South Asian market and the South East Asian market, will give it back its significance. The mess that the region is in, with myriad insurrections pulling in different directions, and a politics that has failed abjectly to be in the driver's seat, is only hastening our own decay with every ticking second. The new epoch needs new issues. The northeast must live up to this expectation and prepare to discard yesterday's slogans and set new political and economic agendas in tune with the modern.

2

RELATIONSHIP BETWEEN THE DRUG-RELATED PERSONAL CHARACTERISTIC OF THE ADDICT AND THE SOCIO-CULTURAL AND ECONOMIC FACTORS

—*S. Romeobala Devi*

Manipur is the state in India, which lies in the North-eastern corner as a hill girt. Manipur has become one of the worst drug affected states in India even today. The problem of abuse has escalated, and is assuming serious social dimension. It is well-known that the entire quality of the drug abused in Manipur comes from across the border from Myanmar side. Being situated close to the Myanmar and Golden Triangle, Manipur has become not only a transit point for drug consumption but also the youths of Manipur in particular, have fallen a victim to drug abuse in a big way.

In fact, drugs from Myanmar enter in Manipur through the passage of Behiang and Moreh both of which are very close to Myanmar. The long border with Myanmar (352 km) has less polices, and as a result of which many drug routes have come up.

Four main drug routes have also so far been identified. These are:

i. Tamu-Moreh-Imphal-Kohima-Dimapur

ii. New Somtal-Sugnu-Churachandpur-Imphal - Kohima – Dimapur

iii. Keinar-Behiang-Churachandpur-Imphal – Kohima – Dimapur and

iv. Somrah – Tulsong – Kharasom –Jessami – Kohima-Dimapur

In addition to these well-identified routes, there are innumerable jungle tracks all of which are used by drug traffickers. Drug abuse refers to the persistent sporadic excessive, often illegal drug use, which occurs in a manner not acceptable to the normal medical practice or to the society. Continuous use of drug leads one to become drug dependent and then drug addict. To be addicted to a drug means to be dependent on it both physically and mentally. The abuser uses the drug with such frequency that it comes physical or mental harm or worsens social functioning.

The Drug Problem and the Common Drugs of Abuse in Manipur

There are many 'drug problems' in Manipur. Illicit use of tranquilizer's, sedatives, sleeping aids, stimulants, etc., creates problems. The use of tobacco (in different forms), caffeine and alcohol by the teenagers and also by the adults is a big problem in Manipur although these materials may be acceptable to some communities as a matter of traditional rights. Still more serious problem is the spread of addiction to what are known as "deadly drugs or hard drugs" (CSD), cocaine, heroin etc. The problems in the use of these drugs caused many harmful effects on the user's body and in the society. Some such harmful effects of the illicit use of drugs on human body may include mental fatigue, dizziness, feeling of fear, day dreaming and confusion, loss of co-ordination, distorted perception, uncontrolled anger; damage of organs and organ systems, reduced sex hormones, increase of blood pressure, pulse rate and heart beat, permanent genetic damage, personality problems; panic and suicidal feelings, and sudden death.

Misuse of drugs affects the smooth functioning of a family. It disrupts economic planning and administration of the state. It also affects almost all aspects of the progress of a nation. The effect of taking drug on the body is unlike any other foodstuff taken by someone for his nourishment. Once a person is hooked to drug, an all-out attempt is made to get more of the drug at any cost. Generally drug addiction begins in a social setting and ends up alone, pondering hopelessly. So, a drug is not fact in relationship with others. Knowingly or unknowingly people stated taking drug of one kind or the other. And so the problem of drug abuse has become a very ancient one, and founded some myths. But people in modern times started acknowledging that the problem of drug menace is a very serious and wide spread one.

Now-a-days several types of drugs are available in the market. Before we proceed to the next step it will be useful to have a bird's eye view of the whole range of 'soft and hard drug', including tobacco and alcohol. In doing this we will be able to place each individual drug in proper context.

Tobacco and alcohol area coincidental to be non-medical drugs, but they are all mind altering drugs.

The Main Drugs of Abuse

Following the Hong Kong Council of Social Science, (1998), most of the drugs of abuse may be grouped into narcotic and non-narcotic drugs:

I) *Narcotic Drugs*:

The narcotic drugs are also known as psychotropic drugs. They are as follows:

i) Opium, ii) Morphine, iii) Heroin, iv) Codeine, v) Pantopan, vi) Methadone, vii) Etorphine,

viii) Pethidine, ix) Oxycordone (Percodon), x) Wellconal, xi) Tilidine and xii) Meperidine (Demerol)

II. *Non-Narcotic Drugs of Abuse*

The non-narcotic drugs include hallucinogens organic solvents and stimulants. All these drugs are no less dangerous than the narcotic drugs if used without medical advice. They are as follows:

i) Hallucinogens

ii) Lysergic Acid Diethylamide (LSD)

 a) Mascaline

 b) Psilocybin and Psilocin

 c) Phencyclohexyl piperidine or phencyclidine (PCP)

 d) DOM (2,3 dimethory-4-methylanaphetamine

 e) MDA (3,4 methylene-dioxyampjetomine)

 f) DET (Diethyltryptmaine)

iii) Cannabis

 a) Marijuana

 b) Harshish

 c) Ganja

 d) Bhang

iv) Organic solvents

 a) Cocaine

 b) Crack

 c) Amphaemines

 d) Preludin

Different drugs have different effects on the body. Illegal uses of them cause irreparable loss to the society and the nation. Many youths in particular, are heavily affected by the misuse of drugs. Drug abusers have become weak, sickly, and are not able to talk up any hardships or, participate in healthy activities. Consequently, many of them physically strong and mentally fit to enable themselves face the challenges of life. When the world is stepping into the 21st century, there shall be considerable demand for fitness from all sections of the people and the level of happiness of the people to a great extent. So, we require eradicating the problems of drug abuse and save the lives of the people from sinking in the pressure of drug abuse.

We are aware that the problem of drug abuse assumed a gigantic proportion. It has disturbed our people, broken the traditional culture and threatened the very existence of this peace loving group of people of this soil. In recent years, the peaceful atmosphere was disturbed by bloodshed, violent and brutal murder as an outcome of drug trafficking. And this little state (Manipur) has been caught the attention of the whole world. Unless a quick and effective action is taken to solve the problems of drug abuse in Manipur, the future of the youths on whom the hope of the nation depends will remain gloomy.

It is well-known that the various dimensions of the problem of drug abuse and the way in which it manifests, we have analyzed the characteristics of drug addicts. We have also examined whether there is also any relationship between the personal characteristics of the drug addicts and socio-cultural and economic factors. The three sets of variables have been formulated as indicators of drug related characteristics and socio-cultural and economic factors. Education, occupation and income of the addict have direct relevance to spelling out the status, capacity, and strength of the individual to take part in his interaction with the society, and also to face any consequences in the process of interaction. We have examined these variables in relation to:

1. Age at first initiation to drugs.
2. Reasons for the first intake of drugs.
3. Duration of drug abuse / addiction.
4. Motivation at the time of admission to the de-addiction centres for treatment and
5. Self-perception on habits of taking drugs.

Relationship of Education with Drug Related Personal Characteristics

Education is a process, which helps in shaping, forming and moulding the behaviour of an individual. Education is the only cure for certain diseases the modern world has engendered. It is important tool in the fight against social ills. It is also considered as a source for socio-economic development. Plato said, "Education is the constraining and directing of youth towards that right reason, which the law affirms, and which the experience of the best of our elders has agreed to be truly right."

1. It is desirous that the first intake of drugs at an early age is more among the illiterates and elementary level educated person and then those who had been educated up-to the secondary or the college level education were likely to take to drugs at a higher age at initiation. It may be stated that formal education cannot be the only weapon to check the problems of drug abuse. We see now-a-days that many educational institutions in Manipur fail to provide congenial study atmosphere to the students and as a result of this students get bored. They find easy means of cutting their leisure time in drug taking habits.
2. All educational programmes, including drug education programmes the students may be applied as a strong defensive force in combating drug menance.

The reason for abusing the drug for the first time has been classified as: peer group pressure, curiosity, family problems, unemployment, frustration and any other reasons.

3. The educational levels seem not to have any bearing on the duration of drug abuse before the addict attends the De-addiction Centres for treatment. In other words, the relationship between the educational levels and duration of drug abuse is remote.
4. The educated persons may be selecting "any other" place for initiation into drugs as these people have wider avenues of interaction than the less educated or illiterate persons.
5. The self-perception that an addict has on his habit of drug apparently has less relationship with the level of education. It is known that the feeling of pride on the drug abuse habit is the least among the illiterates. The education has less influence on the ability of the individual to distinguish right from wrong, particularly in matters of self-inflicting menace like drug abuse. Formal education system as it is prevalent today in the state is not strong enough to help the individual to see correct perspective about the evils of drug abuse, but in a way it is active in thriving aggressive rebellious feelings in the minds of the students who then feel proud on the drug taking habits.

Relationship of Occupational Status and Drug related Personal Characteristics

Both the employed and unemployed are almost equally prone to taking to drug at the social parties. It is apparent that occupational status bears no significant relationship with the place of first abuse of drugs by the addicts. The pattern of drug abuse remains more or less the same irrespective of the occupational status of the addicts.

Relationship of Income Level with Drug-related Personal Characteristics

The manifestation of the menace of drug abuse shows the

effect of wide spread poverty as well as the effect of an affluent society as the west. No significant relationship exists between the income level of addict and socio-cultural variables relevant to the study. Drug abuse does not discriminate the rich from the poor. Addicts with nil income show truculent behaviour much more than those having personal income. Drug abuse or addiction is now a multi-factoral and multifaceted problem. Any addiction launched towards brining solution to the problem will have to be based on sociological, psychological and medical dimensions. The prevention, control and eradication of the drug abuse problem will require a multi-pronged approach toward reduction of both supply and demand and curing of the addicts.

Suggestions

To combat the threat posed by drugs there is the need to tackle the problem in two approaches viz., curative and preventive.

Curative Aspect:

1. For the cure of the addicts, it is necessary that first of all, the addicts are segregated and treatment be given by the doctors for the improvement of their health. To lift their psychological trauma and depression, they require the services of the psychologists, counselor, social workers and love and affection of the parents.

2. For segregation of the addicts, they are not to be kept in the jails, as it gives a stigma in their personality after coming out of the jails.

3. For treatment and rehabilitation of the addicts, they are to be kept in the well equipped De-addiction Centres. The existing Rehabilitation and De-addiction centres in Manipur are to be improved in terms of infrastructure, treatment and other facilities separately for males and females. State Government should set up one De-addiction Centre in every district of Manipur.

4. Education about the menace of drug abuse and health measures to the people is the best vaccines at the present moment. There is urgent need to expand the present knowledge regarding educational preventive and treatment methodologies and techniques to the people.

5. More and more up-to-date research works do different aspects of drug abuse/addiction offering concrete suggestions to the Government are needed.

Preventive Aspect

It may include the following:

1. Awareness about drug is created among the people through the media of posters, TV, newspapers, journals, street plays, drama, cinema and textbooks.

2. Liquor shops should be changed into entertainment clubs and libraries.

3. Well-organized playgrounds, sports clubs for boys and girls must be developed in different localities.

4. Youths are to be provided with adequate facilities for reading, entertainment of useful activities. Cheap and healthy refreshment rooms are so be set up in the town and near the schools and colleges.

5. It is high time that the Government provides productive working avenues for the educated youths of Manipur.

6. Most immediate step is to check the flow of drug in the state. Very strict measures are to be adopted by the Government to check posts at the Manipur Myanmar border.

7. Since the problem of drug abuse has become a global phenomenon, there should be partnership of the Nation, Government and Non-Government organization to fight the challenge of drugs. A collective force of the institutions, individuals in all walks of life is immediately called for.

8. It is the people who are to eradicate the problems of drug abuse. Unless people are sincere and honest, it will not be possible to solve the problem. The integrity, sacrifice, love and the total quality of the people play a very important role in implementing the legislation and checking the flow of drug. For this moral and spiritual education is a must.

In the end, it is emphasized that behind the three focal points of time, past, present and future, there lies the timeless and the eternal. For the cure as well as for the prevention of drug abuse among the youths, attempts are to be made to establish a personal ebullition with the timeless, eternal through the Yoga, Meditation and Spiritual Practice.

REFERENCES

1. Agarwal, B.B., Sethi and Gupta (1976): Physical and Cognitive effects of chronic bhang (Canabis) intake, *Indian Journal of Psychiatry*, 1(1).
2. Agrawal, Anil (1982): *1000 Crime Quiz*, Rupa & Co.
3. Ahuja, Ram (1978): College youth and drug abuse: A sociological study of nature and incidences of drug abuse among the college students in Jaipur (mimeograph), Deptt. of Sociology, Rajasthan University, Jaipur.
4. Ajwani, J.K. (1985): Some psychological correlates of drug dependence, *Indian Journal of Psychiatry*, 12: 23.
5. Chitnis, S. (1974): *Drug on the College Campus*, Tata Institute of Social Science, Bombay.
6. *Drug Abuse in India* (1977): Report of the Committee appointed by the Government of India, Ministry of Health and Social Welfare, New Delhi.
7. Goddwin, D.W., (1981): *Alcoholism*, Oxford University Press.
8. Kalra. R.M. (1955): *Drug Addiction in Schools*, Sterling Publishers, New Delhi.
9. Indain Medical Association, Manipur, 1988.

3

KABP STUDIES ON SAFER PRACTICES OF INJECTING DRUG AMONG THE IDUs, MANIPUR

—*K. Ingocha Singh*

The world today experiences the drug abuses cutting across the caste, creed and class. Manipur, the northeastern state of India cannot escape from the spell of this international problem. The state is also considered the highest prevalence of HIV cases among the Injecting Drug Users (IDUs). The finding of sentinel surveillance conducted in February- March 1997 was between 73.1% and 83% (MACS Report). Outreach intervention work based on Harm Minimization concept has been taken up by some NGOs among the IDUs to curve down the spread of HIV in the state of Manipur. A KABP study on the safer injecting behaviour among the IDUs was conducted and this present paper is the outcome of this study by focusing on the knowledge, attitude, behaviour and practices on safer injection among the injecting drug users of Ward Nos.12, 13, 14,15 and 16 of Imphal Municipal Council of Manipur. The objectives of the study are to understand IDUs, (a) concept and knowledge on safer injecting practices, (b) Perception and belief on the safer injecting practices and (c) Practice of injecting drugs.

A sample of 160 IDUs who are the inhabitant of ward no. 12, 13, 14, 15 and 16 of Imphal Municipal Council of Manipur has been administered for the proposed study. Questionnaire, in depth interview and focus group interview are employed as research tools for the study.

The main findings for the study show that majority of the IDUs falls under the age group of 20 to 29 years with a percentage of 66.87. Out of the total sample 126 are Hindu Meitei and the remaining 34 are Meitei Laining. Most of the IDUs area literate ranging from primary to post-graduate. The highest number of IDUs falls under the higher secondary level of education with a percentage of 35.00. Majority of the IDUs belong to joint family with a percentage of 54.37, which is followed by nuclear type of family with a percentage of 35.62. Out of the total sample of the study, 63.75% are unmarried and 28.12% are married. It is revealed by the demographic data that majority of the sample are unemployed with a percentage of 70.62 and some of the IDUs engage non-salaries jobs with a percentage of 21.87 and a small number of them engages government salaried job with a percentage of 7.50. The IDUs of the studies group belong to the category of family income group of Rs. 5,001 to 10,000 with a percentage of 71.32. 95.62% of the drug users have heard about safer injection practices. While asking about the meaning of safe and safer injections, majority of them cannot ventilate clearly about the common definition of safe or safer injection. Regarding the sources of knowledge of safe and safer injecting practices, 53.75% of them say that they have heard the information from mostly NGO workers and 45.00% from their peer members. Eighty-two pre cent of the sample does not know the concept of harm minimization. But some of them have heard of it. Regarding the knowledge of cleaning injecting equipments, most of the injecting drug users understand it properly. They also understand about the steps and options of cleaning equipments.

The IDUs believe that one should keep his or her equipments for safe or safer injection of drugs. But majority of them hardly practise it because of fear of noticing it by other members of the family. It is also believed that washing the injecting equipments with saliva before injection kills the virus. They also believe that safe and safer injections are the ideal philosophy to prevent the spread of HIV/AIDS.

Regarding the attitude towards the safe or safer injecting behaviour and practice, almost all of them like its concept and philosophy so as to save themselves from the ill effects of using drugs. But as far as the practice is concerned, they say that even if they understand all about the merits of safe or safer injection, many a time they could not apply the steps because of the pain of withdrawal.

Regarding the practices of injecting drugs, most of them did not take hard drugs at the initial stage. But some of them started with the hard drugs at the initiation. The common drugs initiated at first were alcohols, pills, adhesive like solution, dendrites etc. Majority of them did not inject drugs at the time of initiation. Later on, they switched from chasing or sniffing to injection. They also say that once they started injection they never switched back to chasing again. The reasons for injection of drugs are manifolds. Most of them say that it is because of the high price of the drugs. The quantity required for injection and chasing is quite different which means that in injection, they requires less quantity of drugs compared with chasing or other forms of intake. Another reason for taking injection is of its kick. Almost all the injecting drug users say that the kick they experienced from injection is a unique one and no other form of intake is compatible with it. They say that they get drugs from the residences of the peddlers. Sometimes the peddlers and the injecting drug users fix the timing and the place and the business of buying and selling. This situation is in between the peddlers and their trusted clients. Regarding the habit of sharing injecting equipments, many of them still practice it even though they have a clear idea of safe and safer injection. There are many responsible factors for sharing these injecting equipments. They say that one of their friends has a syringe and another friend brings the drugs; therefore they have to share these equipments. If they inject in the peddlers place, they share these equipment provided by the peddlers as they do not carry their injecting equipments due to fear of being caught by police, or other anti-drug groups like anti-drug campaign wings of arm opposition groups, *meira paibis*, local clubs etc.

4

GENDER RELATION AND ITS HEALTH IMPLICATION AMONG WOMEN: MANIPUR CASE

—Jubita Hajarimayum

The paper broadly attempts to delve into the interlinkages between gender relation and women's health focusing on risk factors for Sexually Transmitted Infections (STIs) including Human Immunodeficiency Virus (HIV) within the larger context of gender roles and inequalities in the state of Manipur. Better health and well being of women is closely associated with their overall status. It shows social construction of women's sexuality and their reproductive role in addition to their extra-domestic roles despite active religious and political participation. Various studies in many societies have shown the question of women's status being defined by the roles they play in religious, political and socio- economic affaires and so forth. Interestingly, in a society like that of Manipur, there are age-old records, which have demonstratively shown women's active participation in multifaceted fields viz., economy, religion, polity, culture etc. , however, changing character on the state of women in the society is of significance to know about. There are possible factors which usher in the complex situation of gender relation which include influences of patriarchal ideology, unplanned urbanisation, exposure to media without appropriate and gender sensitive message, breaking down of traditional kins and village community that support more or less gender equality in the society. The patriarchal family is the dominant family type in this region and it is within its institutional framework that descent, cultural reputations, occupational skills, family reputations and aspirations, and property are nurtured. This is done under the hegemony of patriarchy that controls socio-economic, political and ritual powers. Patriarchal ideology eventually incorporates among the general population and in the meanwhile the traditional indigenous community's unique characteristic features that once support gender equality and higher autonomy for women gradually break down.

Many previous contributions have shown the higher status of women in the state. There are recorded cases that testify the commendable roles of women in public sphere in the shapes of women's movements in the state both during the colonial and postcolonial times. To mention, Nupi lan of 1904 and 1939 during colonial rule; Nisha-Band, Meira Paibi, and Anti-ceasefire extension in the state as a result of agreement between NCSN (IM) and Government of India, 2001 in the post-colonial time can be cited. Historically, Manipur has her own unique cultural character that favours active role, higher autonomy and well placement of the womenfolk in the society. Despite all these positive attributes of the womenfolk, many questions undoubtedly germinate which need a further investigation in an attempt to crystaly understand the phenomenon of the women.

Methods of the Study

The present paper is based on the field study carried out among the Meitei women in the reproductive age group, 14 to 45 years of age in the Imphal West District, Manipur.

The study was exploratory in nature. Purposive random sampling method was selected. Total number of 200-questionnaire survey was done - 100 questionnaires from the wives of infected HIV/AIDS/STIs and intravenous drug users (IDUs) and 100 questionnaires randomly taken among the married women of general population. In addition, 30 in-depth interviews; 10 focused group discussion; and 10 key informants interviews including community leaders, health practitioners, experts in the non-government sector in the field of gender and HIV/AIDS/STIs were also done. Ten focused group discussions among the unmarried young girls were also carried out to supplement the findings

Based on the survey, some of the notable arguments, which emerged on the magnitude, and ramifications of gender differentials in women's health can be discussed here:

- Lower socio-economic status
- More vulnerable than men in reproductive and sexual health related problems
- More subject to gender based violence than men
- Inappropriate and less health care facility and health education

Lower Socio-economic Status

The study observed that women's socio-economic status is lower among the Meitei community. Though the status of women in the state is comparatively higher than their counterparts in other parts of patriarchal societies in India, the study reflects women of reproductive age group being characterized by less mobility, more restriction, less economic independence, burden of household responsibility and child caring, and assigned value to dowry.

Even though some women earn money, their expenditure to health priority is minimal, as the priority has been given to families. As narrated, they are educated at least up to graduate or undergraduate but difficulty in getting earning job or any kind of income generating activity. Women have inherited property neither from their paternal families nor husbands. In practice, they have no absolute control over their dowry (aunpot). Only a few women partake traditional income generating works like household industry, weaving, handloom etc. They prefer to work for government or semi-government jobs. This is a tip of the iceberg of the societal preference of valuing government or semi-government sector than traditional ones. As the organized sector is limited, difficulty lies to accommodate all the educated women in it. Corruption aggravates more problems to poorer women in particular. In such situation is seen preference given to the son/sons in education and for paid job in an organized sector in the family with limited resources. This is a phenomenon since the last few decades among the indigenous peoples of Manipur.

Women of reproductive age group narrate that they get less nutritious food despite loss of their extra energy in child bearing, caring and household chores. In the Meitei hindu family, woman eats later after serving husband and family members. She cannot even touch husband's food while eating. In a family with less resource, the social norm of eating after feeding the family members implies women less access to food, less nutrition affecting woman's status and well being.

Gender Inequality and Sexual and Reproductive Health

The study shows negative factors inherent in the conditions governing women's health, which have implications for women more vulnerable to STIs including HIV infection. In Manipur, an indication of alarming situation of the HIV infected women who do not inject drugs has been shown in the last few decades. There are commercial sex workers who fall within the STIs/HIV vulnerable group; a sizeable proportion is infected through heterosexuality largely within the institution of marriage. Most are in asymtomatic phase, unaware that they are infected.

What makes women particularly vulnerable in the context of the growing STIs/HIV epidemic is the state of their social and biological factors associated herein. The inability of women to protect themselves from being infected and reinfected rests on the nature of power relations between husbands and wives in the larger society and its microcosm, the familial set up which contributes the women to vulnerability. If women do not/cannot respond to their husbands' sexual satisfaction, it may become a threat to effective monogamy. This clearly implies that women have less control over their bodies and health. The poorer women's exposure to sexuality make vulnerable to sexual and economic exploitation.

The other dimension of inequality is where men enjoy greater degrees of sexual freedom outside the familial framework, which have serious implications to the health of their wives and sexual partner(s). Women's self-esteem and higher recognition associated with child bearing make women vulnerable whose husbands are HIV/STIs infected. Men's sexual choices and behaviour can affect reproductive health of their wives as well as those of their partners.

Women have unprotected sex. On query, they reveal the size of family dominantly dictated at the wishes of husbands and the families. Exploring further reflects preference to small families but it has been observed that most choices relating to fertility were made on the basis of socio-cultural conventions. Gender relations complicate fertility choice. Women have less say in decision-making regarding the number of children, spacing and sexual timing. They have sex on their husbands' desires. Women who know about their husbands' HIV/STIs risk behaviour cannot ask to use condom or safer sex.

Respondent said:

> "When I gave condom to my husband who is IDU and have multiple sexual partners, he said you are my wife, why should I use it".

For the women who have no knowledge of safer sex, sexual health and rights, condom is the only means for controlling unwanted pregnancy. Women face difficulty to express problems related to reproductive and sexual health to their husbands.

STIs including HIV are increasingly being realized as a major health crisis in Manipur. The health problems of women of reproductive age group are associated with their sexual behavior. The problems include unwanted pregnancy, illegal abortion – the possibility of contacting STIs including infection with HIV. In a patriarchal and gender unequal society, women are socialized to be submissive and not to say 'No". This socialization patterns combine to increase the risk to women when they become sexually active and got married. Many forms of Influence of patriarchal norm and characteristics in the indigenous society of Manipur contribute gender inequality.

Reproductive is a gender issue. It is affected by societal norms and value systems, which indicate ideal behaviour for men and women and determine their different social roles, status and identities. These gender norms vary across cultures. Still women are observed to be subservient to normative patriarchy in most societies.

This is paradoxical to see the burden of reproductive and sexual health related problems of women despite their active roles in domesticity, society, religion, polity and economy. Patriarchal family norms operate differently for men and women in any society.

Gender-based Violence

Occurrences of increased gender based violences - domestic and sexual violences have been observed in Manipur despite national and international movements against any kind of violence against women. There are reported cases of women suicides. There have been cases of sexual and physical violence perpetrated by the state security agencies in the past few decades. The finding reveals women facing domestic violence. Women interviewed expressed ill-treatment meted out to them by the in-laws and other member of conjugal family despite their risk from husbands' exposure to risk behaviour to STIs / HIV. In addition to the risk of STIs/ HIV, Widows of HIV infected or drug related husbands face more violence.

One widow respondent

> "I am sure I might be infected with HIV from my husband but I am scared to know the consequences of blood test. My husband died after two years of my marriage due to HIV/AIDS. I didn't know he was infected before I got married but I knew he was intravenous drug user. My husband's family is false charging me that my husband died due to AIDS infected from me. I am being harassed and mentally tortured. My husband's family wants me to leave the house with my one-year-old daughter".

Poorer women face more violence. Women who have less resources, assets and properties face more violence both domestic and sexual. Women in Manipur are especially vulnerable to the threat of sexual and physical violence due to the militarization in the phenomenon of conflict between the state security agencies and armed opposition to it in the region. In Manipur women groups and community responded to violence against women. Meanwhile, there are many cases of domestic violence and sexual violence in the society that need to be addressed.

Inappropriate and Less Health Facility and Education

Many women feel reluctance to attend the normal public health centers for STIs/HIV because of judgmental attitude of the staff and risk of being seen by relatives. Many health services provided by the state are less known by them. Women who are infected STIs/HIV or develop symptoms of STIs are reluctant to consult doctors. Many women are unaware of the STIs even if they are infected. They came to know only in the late stage.

Information on reproductive and sexual health comes to women through more impersonal communication such as TV, radio, wall posters/writings and from kins and friends. Information they catered is inaccurate. Women particularly unmarried and newly married felt very reluctance to clear their doubt. When women have serious problems of STIs/HIV, difficulty lies to take help from health service providers particularly government health centers as health practitioners have negative attitude towards the women who are suffering from STIs.

Many women face problem with no proper facility for safe abortion of unwanted pregnancy; lack of counselling facility; high cost in the private clinics; and judgemental attitude. Cases of conducting illegal and unsafe abortion by the unqualified and untrained practitioners are seen. This is again a question of vulnerability to women's reproductive and sexual health. Reproductive and sexual health tend to focus only to the married women because of their biological function of childbearing while little attention is given to men and unmarried adolescent and youths in terms of reproductive and sexual health. The existing health service system tends to perpetuate gender disparities in doing so, even though men's concern & responsibilities in this area are influential in couples' decision concerning reproductive and sexual health.

Conclusion

HIV/AIDS/STIs pandemic opens up many related issues impinging on health and well being among the women of Manipur. Most interesting issue arises from the study is the fact that despite international and national women's movements on reproductive and sexual health and active involvement of women in various movements in the state, there is no specific movement on women's health and well being in Manipur in this crucial age of HIV/AIDS/STIs epidemic situation. Reproductive and sexual health is a gender issue.

Increasing rate of HIV/STIs among the women and children shows their lower position, less autonomy, less decision-making power, lack of knowledge on health and rights. Need of the hours is to think of how can traditional Indigenous feature that favours higher autonomy of women can be given a thought along with developing modern universal standards and norms that support women towards ushering in peace, freedom, free of violence, justice and gender oriented development.

Acknowledgements

I acknowledge the contribution of informants in the study. The analysis is entirely based on information furnished during the fieldwork.

REFERENCES

Ahluwalia, B. K, *Social Change in Manipur,* Delhi, 1984.

Chaki Sirkar, Manjushri, *Feminism in a Traditional Society: Women of the Manipur Valley,* New Delhi, 1984.

Anna Pinto, Jubita, Hajarimayum, Community Response to Violence Against Women in Manipur, Paper presented at *IXth National Women's Conference on Women's Studies,* Hyderabad, 2000.

Bimola, Ksh, Manipur Women – a study; In: Sanajaoba Singh (Ed.), *Manipur Past and Present (The Heritage and ordeals of a Civilization),* New Delhi., Vol. I, 1988.

Berer, Marge, Safe Sex, Women's Reproductive Rights and the Need for a Feminist Movement in the 21 st Century, *Reproductive Health Matters,* Vol.8, No 15, May 2000.

Desai, Neera and M. Krishnaraj, *Women and Society in India,* New Deldi, 1987.

Defo. B. Kauti, Effect of socio-economic disadvantages and Women's Status on women's Health in Cameroon, *Social science and Medicine* Vol. 44, No. 7, 1997.

Hajarimayum, Jubita, *"Meitei women in Transition in Manipur,* 1997, unpublished M.Phil dissertation, Centre for social medicine and community health, JNU, New Delhi.

Hangzo C, Chatterjee A, Sarkar S el al. 1997, *Preaching out beyond the hills: HIV prevention among injecting Drug Users in Manipur,* India.

Pisani, Elizabeth, AIDS into 21 st Centuty: Some Critical Considerations, *Reproductive Health Matters,* Vol.8, No 15, May 2000.

Sanamani, Yambem "Nipilan: Manipur women's Agitation 1939", *Economic and Political Weekly,* Vol X, No. 8, 1976.

Salm, Aagje Papineau, promoting Reproductive and Sexual Health in the Era of Sector – Wide Approaches (SWAPs), *Reproductive Health Matters,* Vol.8, No 15, May 2000.

5

DRUG USE AND THE NEED FOR SOCIAL ADVOCACY AMONG ADOLESCENTS

—Salam Irene

The use of mind-altering substances goes back to the first historical records that we have from several early cultures and civilizations. The first Sanskrit texts of ancient Indian civilizations, the hymns and poems of the Vedas, describe the use of a still mysterious agent, soma, which some scholars regard as being hallucinogenic mushrooms, and others, as more likely to have been either an opiate or a marijuana derivative. Marihuana itself is described in the Ayurveda, as useful for poets, musicians, singers, saints and manual labours review of history suggest, that in many cultures and times, mind altering agents sere not only a part of public life, but a significant component of religions and ritual life[1]. Opium is the parent agent of all opiate narcotics, including heroin, a drug of choice for IDUs in Manipur. At the start of the last millennium, it was arguably among the most effective agents mankind had. While the opiates had many medicinal uses, they have probably always been addictive. The historical spread of poppy cultivation into South-east Asia can only be guessed at, but by the time European explores penetrated main and South East Asia from the 1600s onwards, opium was known and was used for its medicinal values. The most significant change in the history, of opiate use came about in the late 18th to 19th centuries and involved interestingly, financial issues raised by another psychoactive agent-tea. Both the British and the Dutch East India companies were involved in the lucrative tea trade, then China's major agricultural export. Tea became more than popular in Europe – the demand for tea was immense, but ching dynasty China had little demand for British goods. China wanted to trade tea for European and British silver. The result was a rapidly growing trade imbalance. Desperate to redress the trade imbalance, and to find a product of interest to Chinese consumers, the British began importing increasing quantities of opium to China. British opium was being grown largely in Indian Bengal then a British Colony.[2]

For China, the results were divesting, opium imports led to what may be one of the world's first and best-documented epidemic of opiate addiction. China banned opium trafficking, but failed to control it. In 1840, China responded to crisis with the famous dumping of 20,000 chests of British opium into the South China Sea. The victory of the British in the first opium war, and the European victory in the second opium war, the dramatic expansion of poppy cultivation in colonial India, and the fortunes made in controlling the shipping and distribution of opium into China, the first great narcotics economy was born. As in China, colonial economic forces (French) created in Laos, another narcotic based economy. While these historical events are well documented, they are little understood, or noted, in today's debate on drug use. Two further interventions were to change the history of opiate use; the syringe and heroin, opium is not an ideal agent for injection, but in the 1930s morphine was methylated adding fat-soluble methyl groups that made the new compound heroin, able to enter the brain more quickly and efficiently. Through 1930s and 1940s, heroin, a pain agent, increasingly left the hospital and moved to the streets.[3]

After World War II, with the collapse of colonial empires and the emergence of communist China, the opium industry in Asia went through profound changes. The defeated remnants of the Chinese Nationalist Army the KMT, Who did not make it to Taiwan, fled into the hills of Northern Burma, and began to develop the Shan, Korang and Wa regions, now so dominant in Asia's heroin trade. The Vietnam War era brought the Asia trade again into world focus. Burma, after General Ne Win's Coup, partnered with the KMT, the supply the growing heroin demand among the United States Forces in Indo-China. The next great change in opium came with the Soviet invasion of Afghanistan. The Afghan resistance, desperate for funds to buy munitions turned to poppy cultivation, using opium to fund their war effort.[4]

Drug use in Asian countries to continues to increase, and new and ever more hazardous and harmful drug use patterns are continuing to emerge. Many use multiple substances, inject in preference to smoking,' chasing' or snorting, share needles, syringe, drug paraphernalia and drug solutions and preparations indiscriminately, and use alcohol and other psychoactive drugs excessively. These drug use behaviours occur in the context of countries in Asia, which are highly affected by HIV/AIDS.[5] But a perspective that dictates that drug free society is the only acceptable objective for drug policy, can impedes strategies that are more accepting of short and intermediate treatment goals.[6] The understanding about the determinants and consequences of drug use and drug dependence is limited. Most explanations put forward about the reasons for drug taking, center upon the notion that drug users fall prey to the bad influence of their peers, stepping drug is regarded as a simple matter of correct information, better life skills, will power and a commitment to changing 'wrong thinking'. It is assumed that addicts will respond positively to coercion or detoxification.[7] It is therefore necessary to identify factors that facilitate change and identify useful opportunities and levers that will result in a more benign/ effective policy towards adolescents vulnerable to, or affected by drug use.

Illegal drug production has undergone globalization over recent decades. With heroin, this has involved the shift of refining to opium growing areas. This transfer of technology took advantage of poorer low enforcement controls and lower production costs. International improvement in transport facilitate the movement and marketing of drugs using well co-ordinated and distribution networks, Injecting forms of drugs are usually more compact that non injectable ones, and therefore easier to smuggle, in turn drug production and trafficking influence the local availability of injectable preparations.[8] Today injecting use has increased in terms of the numbers and the percentages of the participants involved. IDU is rarely known phenomenon in the Indian sub-continent two decades ago. The mid-eighties witnessed an epidemic of heroin injecting in the North Eastern States of Manipur, Mizoram, Nagaland. The early nineties saw a epidemic of pharmaceutical injecting in the major metropolises of Delhi, Calcutta, and Chennai, The clandestine nature of drug injecting makes it a difficult behaviour to survey, using only quantitative tools.[9]

India has a long history of traditional drug use with opium and ganja being the most popular traditional drugs available. Until the early 1980s, opium and ganja were available to registered users from government authorized shops. However, with growing concerns of the International community and the introduction of the NDPS Act in 1985, the users are seeking alternatives. At this time, political events on India's western borders resulted in the Iran-Iraq quantities of semi –refined heroin were being produced on a large scale for export to western countries. As a result large quantities of brown sugar, locally known as smack, began to flood the Indian market for re-export, and a percentage of this became available to the

Indian markets. The mid-80s witnessed large numbers of people in the cities using brown sugar, with many not even knowing its addictive potential until it was too late. Don Des Jarlais et al. point out that drug users are more likely to become injecting drug users if they are in contact with other IDUs. This theory suggest that incidence is not a linear function, but an exponential function, as drug users mix freely with other drug users and learn new behaviours easily. But the social mixing of drug uses is easily distributed by changes to supply and demand and law enforcement. This is likely to be reflected in discontinuities in a graphical representation of the incidence of IDU. It is then reasonable to assume that the incidence of IDU approximates a linear function. Certain events identified in literature have an important bearing on an analysis of IDU.

(1) The rapid diffusion of IDU in the North Eastern States of India.

(2) The NDPA-1985

(3) The establishment of an apex enforcement agency under the Ministry of Finance, Dept. of Revenue, Narcotics Control Bureau, constituted and set up in Delhi in 1986.

(4) The release of injectable buprenorphine in the Indian market in 1987.

(5) The prevention of Illicit Traffic in Narcotic Drugs and Psychotropic Substances Act of 1988.

(6) The several crackdowns on drug supplics following the assassination of Rajiv Gandhi in 1991.[10]

Opiate drug use in India followed two distinct courses since the early 1980s. The Major metropolitan cities of India had witnessed massive spread of heroin smoking in the early 1980s. The predominant pattern of heroin use in the northern states of the country, in contrast was injecting from the beginning. The cost of the dose of the cocktail of pharmaceutical drugs is about Rs.20 heroin costs Rs.50 for about 100 mg while larger quantities area available at Rs. 200-300 per gram.[11] In Manipur the price of heroin fluctuate because of various reasons, like enforcement controls, exchange rate. Indian/Myanmar currency etc. poly drug use is believed to be associated with an increase in drug overdose related deaths. The philosophy of the government is to engage the non-governmental sector in the delivery of dug treatment and rehabilitation services recognising that drug abuse is a psycho-socio-medical problem, which is best, handled by adoption of a community based approach.[12]

There is no accurate data about when opiate and pharmaceutical drug use started in Manipur. Use of drugs such as prodrom, Mandrax, calmpose etc.among the youth started in the early 1970s . In the early 1980s, there was a scarcity of morphine in Imphal and the morphine injectors started using heroin as a substitute. Injecting heroin was more economical than smoking it or chasing.[13]

In the early days of the HIV/AIDS epidemic in Manipur, drug users were the targets of blame and retribution. Police resorted to mass arrest and imprisonment of drug users. Inside the jails, they were placed in leg shackles and subjected to involuntary HIV testing; this practice came to be known as the 'police model'. Many parents themselves contacted the police to put their drug using children in Sajiwa jail. Access to drug treatment was limited. NGOs were running drug De-addiction center under the direct supervision of the ministry of welfare without any dialogue with the ministry of Health, and often offered only an abstinence goal in treatment. The relapse rate was more than 80%. The rapid increase in HIV sero prevalence was attributed to the fact that the policy of harm reduction was not implemented until 1996. Any activities of this nature that were implemented between 1990 and 1996 were conducted only on a small scale by a small number of NGOs. Now there is a clear policy in support of harm minimization.[14] (Harm reduction can be viewed as the prevention of adverse consequences of illicit drug use without necessarily reducing their consumption, It can encompass various aspects of psychoactive drug use, form restricting the advertising of cigarettes to promoting hepatitis vaccination programs for IDUs. There is an emphasis for short-term pragmatic goals over long-term idealistic goals).

This assumes importance when we consider the long and porous nature of the Indo-Myanmar border which touches Manipur (398 km), and the facility of movement without travel documents on either side of the border (up to a certain distance) have led to the growth of smuggling activities on this border. The factor, which creates a very congenial atmosphere for trafficking in drugs, is that the population a long the border is largely tribal with almost all tribes having trans border ethnic congruity. Due to ethnic similarities and mutual inter dependence; the tribals residing on the Myanmar side have had considerable influence and control over smuggling activities. There is substantial production of opium in Myanmar and a number of heroin refineries.[15]

The link between illegal drug use and AIDS is becoming a serious concern of the government in the region since it is devastating a affecting the social fabric of the community and Asian values, It is also damaging the credibility of the states because drug trafficking caused a lot of corruption and contempt for the law in areas where drugs area produced and trafficked, We have to be very careful and pragmatic in our policy in order to apply proper responses to the challenge that we have. It is important that the response to drug issues should not pose another threat to the community. IDU are critical to the spread of HIV/AIDS. The risky habit of sharing needles and other injecting paraphernalia has been acknowledged as the most efficient, fastest and convincing way of transmitting HIV/AIDS. This assumes great significance for a state like Manipur, located along major drug trade route.

Currently adopted low enforcement and supply reduction strategies may have contributed to the shifts in drug use and methods of administration from those that posed less public health hazard to those posing grater hazard. Current drug policy is to reduce availability of drugs through the narcotic drugs and psychotropic substances Act of 1985. The Act as one of the most severe Acts in the Indian Penal Code, was intentionally harsh, as it was constituted to avert drug cartels form conducting their affairs in India. The implications of the Act were that petty drug users and peddlers were given harsh sentences, while the real culprits somehow managed to escape the dragnet. A continuous process of advocacy resulted in revision of the act in 2001, making the penal code related to drugs use more realistic and benign.

Morphine and pethidine injecting began in Manipur in the 1970s. From the early 1980's heroin became the illicit drug of choice. Over the past few years spamoproxyvon has increasing been injected its effect is short lived, lasting less than 60 minutes, so among IDUs it is often injected 5-7 times per day. In 1990, it was estimated that there were 15-20,000 IDUs in Manipur, second estimate in 2001 suggested that there were 14,000 IDUs in Imphal district alone, of these, it is estimated that 5-10% are female. The one study of female drug users in Manipur(1997) found them to be at high risk of HIV; prevalence among the female IDUs. Although the number of female IDUs involved in sex work is small, they can contribute disproportionately to an HIV/AIDS epidemic. There is considerable reluctance among female IDUs to purchase needles and syringe form pharmacies, or procure them free form RIAC, for fear of disclosure and identification as drug injectors. Until recently condom use even among sex workers was infrequent, and the problem remains of ensuring regular use among all those injectors, male /female who can transmit both HIV and STIs. An overlap of risk behaviours, especially among adolescents, require an urgent and innovative response

- it is here that social advocacy can play a pivotal role, as prevention is better than cure.

The Need for Social Advocacy among Adolescents

An adolescent may progressively spend more time with users where she/he experiences a greater sense of security and comfort, absent at home at school or college for parents to assume a dictatorial posture is less, as it results in meaningless skirmishes, with no solution, or undesired results. Parents need to make continuous efforts to understand what appeals to their children; for instance in music, dress, food etc., even though it may appear undesirable to the parent, it appeals to a teenager, One this is established and understood, it opens up communication channels between both. If a parent empathizes with the child she/he would be more open to suggestions. Both sides must understand that it is important to arrive at an appropriate code of behaviour, fostered by a sense of self-discipline, so as to endure that teenagers become responsible as they grow up. Make the effort to share your child's life informed about what subjects she/he likes and dislikes, who sits next to her/him in the classroom, and who's her/his best friend asserts Dr. Anukant Mittal (Psychiatrist, Mumbai).

The necessity for maintaining open channels of communication is evidence from the practice given below:

A new trends among adolescents in Imphal is not the injecting of licit/illicit drugs, but the injecting of the liquid center of chewing gums, popular among high school students. A s the injected substance is not a drug the adolescents injecting it, don't perceive the necessity of precaution and share needles/ syringes. Young girls indulging in this risk behaviour are teenagers, just becoming conscious of their sexuality, who see the sharing of injecting equipment as a symbol of bonding, a token of their affection for their male partner. The injecting of chewing gums occurs at the sites of tutorial centers, which offer coeducational teaching in different discipline, to adolescents, in classes ranging from 7-12. Because of frequent disturbances in the academic calendar, absence of regular classed in many schools, parents' area constrained to send their children, mostly unescorted to these tutorial centers. These centers become unregulated meeting places for adolescents. Most of them posses some knowledge of the means of transmission of HIV, but in the first flush of attraction to the opposite sex, both teenage girls and boys place themselves at risk. Among them, pre-marital sex is on the increase, and teenagers uninitiated in sexual activity, afraid to ask for advice, afraid to purchase condom, for fear of their actions coning to the knowledge of their parents, do not practice safe sex. They are at risk of HIV, STDs, unwanted pregnancies and abortions. Pregnancy sometimes culminates in early marriage, which soon degenerates into constant sparring. The young husband graduates to harder drugs and even sells his wife's wedding jewelry to sustain his growing drug habit, leaving the young adolescent wife with no economic security. Early marriage usually disrupts the couple's school education, and the couple has access to no sustainable sources of livelihood. The situation is exacerbated with the birth of children, as this places great financial strain on the young couple.

When a child attains poverty, he/she begins to distance himself/herself from parents and family. Adolescents become aloof and secretive and parents are often at their wit's end trying to maintain a channel of communication with their offspring. Although parents feel hurt and left out, it is imperative that they make all our efforts to maintain even limited communication with their teenage children. Today, society is in transition, and traditional joint families are being displaced and replaced by nuclear families, where both parents work and therefore have less time/energy to devote to their children. However, because of increased affluence resulting from a combination of income of both parents, many such parents believe that as they have enrolled their children in reputed centers of learning an also arranged tuition in almost all subjects in tutorial centers of excellence they are absolved from overseeing/or taking interest in the day to day, learning / school activities of their children, what parents tend to overlook is the fact that the endless routine of waking up even before dawn, fitting in tution before school, then again after school, puts tremendous pressure on teenaged children. Many such children because of constantly repeated refrains on the necessity and importance of studying by parents / elders, and lack of sufficient recreation time to unwind, take not only an intense dislike to studying, but develop increasing animosity towards their parents. This makes them vulnerable to peer pressure and vulnerable to drug use. Moreover, most teenagers especially boys are possessed of a restless energy, like a locomotive halting at a station, but ready to leap forward in a moment. Teenagers are also possessed great curiosity and are not afraid to experiment or indulge in rash or risk behaviour. Under the influence of drugs, many adolescent boys manipulate/ coerce teenage girls into unsafe sexual behaviour. Moreover teenage boys are afraid to purchase condoms because of fear of detection from family / society, or are afraid to carry condoms when out on a date, because the girl will suspect the intentions of the boy, and will refuse to date him. Parents, teachers, community workers must build emotional bonds, cultivate sincerity and compassion in children 9instead of competition) and foster understanding. Children are often looked upon as objects or assets who are tutored what to say / do, from the time of the pre-nursery interview onwards, through their parents' aspirations (to come first in class, to pursue a career as a doctor, engineer, government employee), set chains around them. Instead of fostering creative talent, a child and especially adolescent are forced to score more and more marks in adolescents are forced to score more and more marks in not one, but all subjects. In the end, they wind up disliking not only studies, but their parents as well. To remove this coercive pressure, teenagers often find solace in drugs.

Unfortunately drug use is addictive usually, not it is difficult for the adolescent to get off the roller coaster ride. For drug users are way ahead in finding ways of using /accessing drugs.

As harm reduction aims at reducing drug related harm without requiring abstention from drug use, many people believe that prohibition paradigm, would be at stake. But harm reduction does not seek to replace abstinence oriented strategies/ paradigm, but to complement them. Harm reduction is pragmatic, effective and cost effective. Besides preventing HIV/AIDS, Hepatitis C, it reduces problematic drug use by subscribing substitution drugs (e.g. Buprenorphine/ methadone), or altering the modes of intake of substances (e.g. Oral use). It helps to reduce control, the use of drugs in general, and supports the reintegration of drug users into society. Repressive policies on the other hand, do not eliminate the demand for drugs. It is not enough to wait for young people to get involved in drug use, and then try to convince them not to inject. Fear and embarrassment discourage, impede, parents of user from seeking help, causing adolescent users to scale up their intake. Adolescent we all know, get thrills from high risk behaviour.

There are two approaches to drug use – the classic approach focuses on the spread to the disease – addiction, and abstinence is the key in rehabilitating users (Psychiatrists have had a major hand in this idea of addiction and developing epidemiological focus: drug use as deviant behaviour. In the post-modern approach, Harm minimization is the buzzword. Drug use is a social issue that is culturally shaped into a social problem. Professional experts are needed as much as drug users themselves (the lay experts), to manage one's drug use is a deeply embodied experience – ask any problem drinker who has the shakes, or a heroin addict in withdrawal. Self control which all normal bodies experience becomes for the drug user an overwhelming, ongoing problem. While society views users' need for drugs as lack of control, male users as they risk drug taking, comply with what has been called 'hegemonic masculinity'. Female users risky drug taking is about enacting norms of feminine conformity, to be sexually appealing, to relax, or to deaden the pain of abusive relationships. Drugs are regarded as a 'boy's thing' even if the experimentation rates are similar. The people running it, dealing in it, and the people doing the most drugs are boys. Girls may try one something, which will be enough for them. Harm reduction when adopted should embedded empowerment, respect, confidence and self-esteem into adolescent users, and the idea underlying the strategy, must be tolerant and compassionate care by givers. All users engage in risk relationship, and love and intimacy, play a large part in managing these relationships. Unprotected sex can be intentional, negotiated activity, taken to defend the security of relationships and shared destiny with partners, regardless of HIV status. Current research found that women more than men rationalized unprotected sex. Saving one's relationship, rather than one's body, took priority. For female users, their abused bodies are relational investments[16].

Gender Perspective - The conventional disease model of addiction is based on the premise that addiction is a biological, progressive and permanent disease. Harm reduction recognizes that historically people have always sought ways to chang consciousness through use of drugs, that the line separating illegal and legal drugs is culturally constructed, and has nothing to do with inherent dangerousness, and most important, is premised on the acceptance of drug use and drug users. Adolescent girls who use illegal drugs are often stereotyped as more immoral, and out of control, than their male counterparts, as they are not conforming to conventional, specific gender roles. Historically, it has been impossible to just say 'no to drugs'. We need to move towards a world where our understanding of drug use is socially and culturally based, rather than radicalized, sexualized, medicalized and decriminalized. What is required is a supportive and caring environment.[17]

What is the problems adolescent girls experience in their relationship with an addicted partner? It takes a long time before they fully realize that a drug problem really exists. When they try to discuss this with the partner, he denies or plays down the situation. They try to hide the problem from friends, and family, out of fear and shame. They isolate themselves, and fear, insecurity, self-doubt, beset them. This results in a 'relationship addiction' – someone who lets herself be influences by someone else's behaviour, and who is obsessed with controlling that behaviour. Co-dependency is itself a personality disorder – co-dependents have difficulty in experiencing feelings of self-esteem, maintaining functional boundaries, experiencing and acting out their own reality, and taking care of their own feelings. The SELF in relation school assumes that the self of women develop differently from that of women. A popular opinion is that women seek intimacy, while men are focused on sexuality and independence. Men develop by separating themselves by stages (as a child from the mothers, as an adolescent from the family, as an adult from mentors). With self-developments in relationships – women do individualize – they develop their own identity and their own skills, in mutual involvement and empathy. Feelings of fear, anger, confusion, are a logical result, when concern expressed about the relationship meets with denial or trivialization. This creates in adolescent girl/women, a feeling of loss and inadequacy. This sometimes has a crippling effect – the fear that taking action will do more harm. There is a tendency to bear the responsibility for relationships that fail-leading to depression. Girls and young women have to be taught to handle tensions and conflicts in relationships better. When it comes to communication, they can learn to adequately express their feelings and wishes. They must learn that responsibility for drug use, lies with the user, and assertiveness on their part, is different from power.[18]

Social advocacy requires that innovative and appropriate interventions are put in place. Provision of qualified counselors in schools, imparting of sexual education without embarrassment by trained personnel could be a first step. Career counseling, parent-counselor-student interaction, periodic talks by drug counselors, constructive channeling of the dynamic energy of adolescents, interschool competitions, school camps and excursions will stop many adolescents from experimenting or getting hooked on drugs. Because today children in classes 5 and 6 are experimenting by sniffing glue, thinner, nail polish remover, dendrite etc. we have all a responsibility to prevent them from moving on to hard drugs, harming themselves, their families as also the community. We parents cannot direct all our emotional energies towards only our work, where we are obsessed with excellence – we cannot scatter what drugs are left, tiredly around our personnel relationships. Our children shouldn't feel lucky only when we stop nagging them to study, study, and study. We must not push our children to high-risk behaviour, because we lack time/energy/inclination to be 'Really there' when our children need us. Instead let us direct and guide them making the right choice at the appropriate time. The road to recovery for an adolescent user is slow, painful, lonely and unachievable without the support and belief of loved ones. Moreover social or peer pressures far outweigh the fear of parental reaction.

REFERENCES

1. Salam Irene – Interventions by women for women drug users – Makhais Seminar – Ref – *A Brief Historical Overview* – Chris Beyrer
2. *Ibid.*
3. *Ibid.*
4. *Ibid.*
5. AHRN – *The Hidden Epidemic.*
6. Drug Use and HIV Vulnerability – Task Force on Drug Use and HIV Vulnerability.

7. *Ibid.*
8. The rapid Assessment and Response Guide on IDU-WHO
9. RSA of IDU-Delhi-SHARAN.
10. *Ibid.*
11. Drug Use and HIV Vulnerability, *op.cit.*
12. *Ibid.*
13. RSA – Imphal 1999-2000, Kripa Society.
14. Drug Use and HIV Vulnerability, *op.cit.*
15. Brief on Smuggling, D. Imty-N.E. Customs Prevention.
16. Women and Substance Abuse, Elizabeth Ettore, Prof. of Sociology, University of Plymouth, U.K.
17. In the Name of Harm Reduction – Repression and Control, Susan Boyd, Department of Sociology, Halifax, Canada.
18. Towards a new concept in Co-Dependency, Dr Anja Bouman, *IHRA women and Drugs Magazine.*

6

A PERSPECTIVE ON DRUG ABUSE AMONGST YOUTHS IN MANIPUR

—Chitra Ahanthem

Let me start by thanking the Ereima Gender Empowerment and Resource Center (EGERC) for giving me this opportunity to share some of my experiences and concerns in relation to the issue of drug use in Manipur.

When we talk about drugs we will find that they have been in existence all over the world right before the beginning of civilization, even going to mythological roots of different cultures and religions. What are the reasons then that make us look today, at the issue of drug use or abuse, as the case may be, as one that causes alarm?

Three factors contribute significantly towards drug abuse as a major area of concern:

- consequences of drugs on health
- consequences of drugs on society
- consequences of drugs on the economy

Consequences on Health

There are different effects on the health of a person according to the type and mode of drugs used over a period of time. It would take a medical person to state the effects of certain drugs on the health of a person though the most common and obvious consequences are drug dependence, chronic addiction, neurosis and other psychological effects, HIV/AIDS and other blood borne disease infection including Hepatitis C, for which there are yet no treatment facilities in the entire North East region.

Consequences on Society

— Increasing number of school/college drop outs.

— Incidences of petty crimes (for covering the cost factor of using drugs)

— Dysfunctional family units (tension within family structure due to drug use) conventional treatment services (earlier jail/lock up) by sending to rehabilitation centers which gives cause for resentment in case of relapse.

— Indirect effect on women and children: earlier, the myth attached to drug use as a "behavior problem" led many parents to encourage early marriages in the belief that it would give a sense of responsibility and stability. Over the years, married IDUs have left behind their wives and children infected by HIV/AIDS or affected financially by their long term treatment of drug use or other diseases or infections. On a more serious note, the widows of IDU's have been left unskilled and at a young age, thereby putting them at a disadvantage regarding jobs for sustaining themselves and their family and vulnerable to exploitation.

— Sporadic and short-term immediate responses to drug use which may not be the need of the hour or situation. For example, the so called "punishments" meted out by Meira Paibi, local clubs and various pressure groups in the form of physical harassment, tonsuring of heads, parading in public, stints at jails and lock ups and even bullet injuries have not been able to make people give up drugs but has only served to make drug users go underground and go ahead with risky behavior like sharing injecting paraphernalia which fuels the HIV/ AIDS epidemic and make it a difficult job for those giving drug related services to reach out to them.

Economic Consequences

There has been no study taken up so far to study the economic impact of drugs on a state or society but if we were even to take an estimate of the drug user population of Manipur as a modest 40,000 and keep the amount of money spent on drugs per person daily as Rs. 50, the total expenditure on drugs would come to Rs. 20,00,000 every day. If we take up calculating further on a monthly and yearly scale, the financial costs of drugs would be a colossal amount.

The estimate of the cost factor involved due to drug use would also include the various treatment costs (medication, accessing treatment facilities etc. including institutional treatment at rehabilitation centers), which only add to the huge amount of money that goes towards addressing the issue of drug abuse today.

Another area that has not been estimated at all is the effect of drugs on the productive levels or output of the work force. Since there are health consequences, it goes without saying that there are bound to be numerous sick leaves and even lay offs which in turn affects the work performance of workers/ employees.

Findings of a Survey

A Rapid Situation Assessment of Drug Use in Imphal (1999-2000) under the auspices of UNESCO, United Nations Drug Control Program (UNDCP) and Ministry of Social Justice and Empowerment (MSJE) took a sample size of 308 drug users from Imphal East and West districts. The sample size also included 30 female drug users.

It was found that 62% of the sample size started using drugs in the age group of 15-19 years; 21% in the age group of 20-24 years; 12 % being under 15 years; 3% in the 25-29 year category and a mere 2% started using drugs after reaching 30 years of age. Sixty four per cent started by drinking substances like alcohol, cough syrup etc.; 19% start with oral use of pills (Nitrosun, Nitrazepam, Zolam, Relipin, Diazepam, Mandrax, Prodrom, Vallium, Hyptozen); 12% start with smoking/chasing while a mere 5% start with direct injecting of Morphine, Heroin, SP etc.

It should be noted that the mode or type of drug used at the initiation period did not necessarily remain the same as most drug users tend to experiment with more "high" and "hard" drugs.

But why do young people, the ones we call the pillars of the future of our society take to using drugs? More pertinent, however, is the issue over what can be done.

Why do Young People take to Drugs?

Universally, young people are known for their zeal, their drive, their enthusiasm. But mostly, the young are also known to be reckless. They want to experiment and seek out new things. And in Manipur where there are not too many avenues for young people to experiment, they pick up the one most open to them: drugs; through influence of external forces/ pressures (environment, friends etc.)

Some other reasons are:

- — Lack of guidance/counseling services for youths, be it health oriented or career oriented.
- — Lack of recreational spaces/hang-outs due to the law and order situation.
- — The pervasive "frustrating/suppressed" environment fostered by the law and order situation; lack of freedom of choice for even cinemas to TV channels.

— The future of unemployment.

— The gap-holes in the education system that is driven by the culture of mass copying and easy examination results through National Open School systems.

— Family structures today, with communication lines between parents and children and spending quality time being major issues.

— Media portrayal of drugs: the use of various intoxicants and drugs by popular movie stars, musicians and others in the world of glamour build up a negative image that reinforces the image of drug use as the "in" thing to do.

— Lack of knowledge about the adverse consequences of drugs also leads young people to taking them up. Day in day out, they are fed up with the idea that "using drugs are not the proper thing to do", but until and unless we respect their ability to grasp and understand how and why drugs "are not the proper thing to do", they will continue to rebel.

— Lack of access to treatment: Various Non Governmental Organizations and Government agencies have taken up measures for giving services to drug users in the form of Needle Syringe Exchange Program, outreach, peer education etc. which form part of what is known as Harm Reduction initiatives. From the Government side, we see them funding rehabilitation centers where there are 15 treatment slots/bed capacity for a treatment duration of 3-6 months. In most instances, the cost of treatment is another area of concern for drug users seeking treatment and the practical issue of young people not being too enthusiastic about the rigid discipline and the long term treatment subjected in a centre. Even when we strictly go by the existing

Harm Reduction initiatives in Manipur (NSEP, outreach, peer education etc.), the success or failure of the service delivery depends on community support or reaction.

What Can be done?

— Call for formulating a drug policy that takes the views and considerations of drug users.

— Include a youth friendly clause/recommendation in the said drug policy.

— Include drug education and awareness in school curriculums starting from the class VIII standard.

— Formulate a plan of action by initiating a multisectoral alliance to give the correct message about drugs and their effects and what services are available for their treatment.

— Call for more comprehensive treatment measures as it is time to move on from old approaches.

— Facilitate ownership towards drug use as a public health concern and a right-based perspective.

REFERENCE

Rapid Situation Assessment, 2000- UNESCO/Kripa Society.

7

DRUG-ABUSE: ISSUES FOR DEVELOPMENT

—E. Bijoy Kumar Singh

Introduction

Gone are those days when drug-abusers used to be dismissed as idle and good-for-nothing fellows. Drug-abuse is no longer a personal problem. Its ramifications began to be considered seriously once intravenous injection of drugs has been found to be a major transmission mechanism of HIV in Manipur. Drug-abuse is associated with many issues including development issues. Drug-abuse can affect economic development and the latter can also affect drug-abuse. The purpose of this paper is to discuss in the context of Manipur the contour of the interaction between drug-abuse and economic development.

Drug-abuse in Manipur

The Committee on Prevention of Drug Abuse (COPDA), I.M.A., Manipur State Branch conducted a survey of drug abuse in Manipur and the epidemiology of Heroin abuse in Manipur in 1988 (June-Dec.) over 45 villages/wards in all districts of Manipur with a Sample size of 18092. It was one year before the first HIV positive case in Manipur was detected. The commonly abused drugs were heroin, alcohol, diazepam,

Chlordiaze poxide, Codiene and antihistamine in cough syrup. Some of the finding of the survey were as follows:

(*i*) There is no significant variation in the number of abusers between urban and rural areas.

(*ii*) Alcohol is more commonly abused by persons above the age of 30 years, Heroin abuse in the age group 20-30 years and cannabis by person above 40 years of age.

(*iii*) The mean age of first drug abuse is 21.8 years.

(*iv*) The percentage of abusers increases with the increase of educational level and maximum number is observed among the high school and college educated people.

(*v*) There is no variation of abuse pattern over different types of occupation.

(*vi*) Around 75% of abusers are active abusers.

(*vii*) Eight two per cent of heroin abusers are using I.V. route.

(*viii*) Drug-abuse has no significant relationship with family or individual income.

(*ix*) Heroin is most commonly abused by the students and unemployed persons. Alcohol is abused commonly by farmers and the employees.

No other survey of comparable nature has been taken so far. In the last 15 years the various dimensions of the problem might have undergone significant changes. Currently the focus is no longer on drug-abuse; it is on HIV/AIDS and their epidemiology. Manipur with hardly 0.2% of India's population contributes nearly 11.44% of India's total HIV positive cases. The top three in descending order are Maharashtra, Tamil Nadu and Manipur. However, the sero-prevalence rate of

Manipur is at least 6 times higher than that of Maharashtra and 20 times higher than that of Tamil Nadu. The age of 72.52% of the HIV positives in Manipur are less than 30 years. The HIV/AIDS epidemic is no longer confined to the injecting drug users (IDUs). It is now spreading among women and children.

The relationship between drug-abuse and development need not be a one-way affair where development may impact on factors leading to drug-abuse. However, this aspect is generally ignored due to the long-term nature of this process. Drug-abuse is one of the human responses to uncertainty and stress and strain of modern life. When development lessens the uncertainty and the stress and strain of modern life the pattern of drug-abuse is also likely to change. On the other hand, the impact of drug abuse and its associated ills on development can be studied in terms of indicators of development and determinants of economic growth, the necessary condition for development.

Indicator of Development

For quite sometime economists have been very uncomfortable with the level of per capita income as a measure of development. There would have been no problem if there were rigid links between economic production (as measured by income per head) and human development (reflected by human indicators such as life expectancy or literacy, or achievements such as self-respect). But these two sets of indicators are not very closely related. The situation improved with the introduction of Human development index, which reflects achievements in the most basic human capabilities leading a long life, being knowledgeable and enjoying a decent standard of living. The three variables representing those aspects are life expectancy, educational attainment and income. Zambia is an extreme case where the effects of HIV/AIDS on life expectancy led to a 4% decline in HDI between 1975 (0.453) and 1997 (0.431). The chances of drug-abusers in

Manipur graduating to HIV positive cases are high due to rampant sharing of syringe and needles contaminated with HIV. Once they become HIV positive, any opportunistic infection can result in full-blown AIDS case. Though little is known about the average incubation period in Manipur, 10 years may be a reasonable guess. It is the upper limit for sub-Saharan countries characterized by abject poverty. The preponderance of youth among Heroin abusers, the high HIV/AIDS risk group, will manifest itself in declining life expectancy. The treatment for managing HIV infection is very costly. At the family level cutting back on all other expenditures including education and health of other family members can finance the treatment of a family member. Only a small proportion of income will be available for standard of –living enhancing activity. At the macro-level if the government finances the treatment by subsidizing hospital and related costs, many other deserving expenditure heads have to be sub-optimal given the overall resource constraints both at the state and central level. Besides the high cost of treatment, there is also the issue of discrimination and social stigma. Thus, drug-abuse in Manipur, if allowed to proceed as it is, is going to impact any development indicator very adversely. Life expectancy will fall, quality of education will deteriorate and income will effectively decline.

Development Issues

Capital and labour are two key components of economic development via their impact on economic growth. Thus, the contour of the impact of drug abuse on development may be viewed via its impact on capital formation both physical and human.

Manipur is poor even by the standard of Indian states. There is no major industry and it is essentially an agrarian economy. Except for the 80,000 or so government employees majority of the workers are in the unorganized sector. Products from the mainland dominate the domestic market. Local entrepreneurs who have made it big are few and they are out competed by mainland industries in terms of access to market, quality of goods and finance. In other words, there is very limited scope for investment of savings into socially productive activities.

The vicinity to the porous boundary with Myanmar and the infamous Golden Triangle gives ample scope to local traders for indulging in lucrative illegal trade in contraband items including heroin, small arms etc. The inadequate development of infrastructure both physical and financial has aborted any impulse for socially productive investment. The emergence of easy money syndrome has adversely affected the work environment. Very little of our economic growth is attributable to domestic saving. Not only our per capita income is low, our expenditure is also appropriated largely by unproductive activities. Thus, though the likely diversion of savings may not have impacted immediately on the level of economic growth, it keeps on delaying the development of a robust linkage between domestic savings and economic growth. The threshold beyond which such a linkage appears keeps receding. For a small sub-national economy like Manipur, there is bound to be a limit to socially unproductive investment. The picture will be slightly different if the treatment cost is absorbed by the state through subsidies and grants. In general, the negative impact of AIDS on average growth in per capita income increases with the share of AIDS treatment costs financed from personal savings and with the skill level of infected workers. Savings diverted by AIDS treatment depend on number of workers, proportion of HIV positive workers, Proportion of HIV positive workers with AIDS, annual treatment cost of AIDS and proportion of treatment cost from savings. The percentage reduction in capital stock each year due to AIDS treatment depends directly on proportion of HIV positive workers, proportion of HIV positive workers with AIDS, average medical costs for AIDS treatment,

GDP per capita proportion of treatment cost from savings and inversely on capital output ratio. In general AIDS reduces the rate of growth of per capita income below, which it would be without AIDS.

Rampant drug-abuse will lower capital accumulation by inducing reallocation of private and public resources from saving investment to medical treatment, social support payment for orphans etc. This will unnecessarily delay the maturing of indigenous development impulse.

Drug-abuse patronizes on illegal parallel economy. It is estimated that drugs worth several thousand crores of rupees are smuggled across the international border. It becomes a big leakage in the normal process of circulation of money and it has a tendency of increase. The increasingly lucrative transactions in the block economy lead to gross misallocation of resources.

Labour that is skilled in production, labour that can operate sophisticated machinery, labour that can create new ideas and new methods in economic activity – is human capital. It is deliberately accumulated and is not just the out- come of population growth or exogenously specified technical progress. Any reasonable description of the growth process must include endogenous components such as the accumulation of human capital. Japan's phenomenal growth in the post world war II period is consistent with the implications of the endogenous growth theory as reflected in the relatively high stock of human capital.

Human capital formation in Manipur has not been impressive due to a general overall decline in the quality of education. Though the literacy rate is high, the quality of education is sub-standard. Education, particularly at the school level, has become a lucrative business leading to mushroom growth of English schools of questionable quality all over the state. Though these schools create jobs for the educated unemployed, the deteriorating quality of education is compounded.

In Manipur the impact of drug-abuse and its associated ills on the level of mortality rate gets confounded with deaths due to insurgency. Though we see the devastating effect of drug-abuse on families, it is not yet visible at the state level. The negative impacts of drug-abuse on population growth however may be more than compensated for by the likely tendency of parents to have larger number of children to ensure that their children survive in their old age. High mortality of the youth in their prime age will prompt risk-averse parents to have more children than parents facing high infant mortality. Mortality of this type has serious implications for investment in education. In the case of high infant mortality, parents are spared of the burden of investment, which is eventually wasted. When parents have to support children who are likely to die in the prime of their youth, they have to reallocate their resources very thinly. Thus, while the size of the work force may remain stagnant, there may be substantial deterioration in quality which may be equated with having less number of workers.

Given the high unemployment rate in bigger states, the shortage of manpower may be easily made up by migrant workers. Earlier migrant workers used to be confined to professions like barber, cobbler and porters. Now they have branched out into new avenues like construction and trade. However, the net contribution of migrant workers to general development of the state will be much less than that of resident workers. The migrant workers now are in a position to dictate the wage-rate at a level considered to be non-remunerative by the local people. This has led to substantial loss of job opportunities for the indigenous labour force.

Conclusion

Thus, drug abuse and its associated evils may adversely affect dynamic factors behind economic growth and distribution of income. The debilitating impact on human capital formation also affects the potential of physical capital. The prospect of technological progress making up this negative impact is also dim in the backdrop of low human capital formation.

REFERENCES

Cuddington, John (1993), "Modelling the Macroeconomic Effects of AIDS, with an Application to Tanzania.

Cuddington, John (1993), Further Results on the Macroeconomic Effects of AIDS, The Dualistic, Labour – Surplus Economy.

Ministry of Health & Health Welfare (1976), *Drug Abuse in India: Report of an Expert Committee*, New Delhi.

Singh, A.D.,(1992) " Survey of Drug Abuse in Manipur", Indian Medical Association Manipur State Branch.

Singh, B., (2001), Drug Abuse and Aids Menace, J.C. Thomas & Others (2001), *Manipur: Constraints in Development of Manipur*, Regency Publications, New Delhi.

The World Bank Economic Review, Vol. 7, No.2, May.

The World Bank Economic Review, Vol. 7, No.3, September.

8

YOUTH, DRUG AND DEVELOPMENT: SPADING LINKAGES

—*H. Sudhir*

A very indispensable parameter of development framework is the need for building up a specified social base and to the nurturing of values and attitude of a secure society. Taking note of it, the paper attempts to lay a hand on the question of social development in this region more specifically Manipur state concerning the youth's drug addictive behaviour and to track down the social values that back up the social development.

Closeness to the famous Golden Triangle and the porous geo-political character facilitated drug trafficking creating an inflow of drug substances and easier entrance to it by the youth irrespective of sexes and class-cultural varieties. The history of drug abuse and HIV/AIDS among the intravenous drug usage, and subsequent transmission of the disease through unsafe sex, mother to child transmission shows a sign of a fragile social security. From being a transit center in the widely profitable overseas drug marketing, the state started showing a serious concern since the early 80s when there began an addictive trend among the youth. Productive social growth could be impeded for the reason that an identified social group as a pillar of overall development began drowning in the wave drug addictive behaviour gearing up near the question of a social breakdown; hence there is an urgent need for a pragmatic approach and initiative to effectively address the issue.

Conceptual Setting

An emergent framework in the study of development that is very much current in the global development exercise is the social perspective. For example, the UN Human Development Reports recognize human factor to the development measurement. This is theoretical articulation that could well be conceded as social sector of development displaying a linkage between social sector and development question. Put in another shape, it articulates that development is based on building up of a strong social sector. The question of social development in the paper is discussed in the way of social impact emerging from drug abuse and its subsequent HIV/AIDS endemic among the youth in the region. The youth group in the paper is used mean the 'most promising-productive' social section in the 15-35-age cohort.

Problem

The interrelation of HIV/AIDS epidemic and development index has been studied in Ethiopia and Sub-Saharan Africa. This framework seems a new one in the Northeast India, which is plagued by the endemic from past few decades. Perceiving the importance, the paper would be a small attempt to touch upon the area. Despite initiatives, which have been taken in different capacities, one area that seems to be kept aside towards a successful response to the epidemic is research orientation. Writing the paper senses the lack of literature and proper documentation. This paper is attempted based mostly on the secondary data gathered from the governmental and non-governmental resource centres. Even the available literature having accessed in writing the paper are mostly of general information types and devoid of specific points, which the paper hunts for. For example, there is no encounter of data on mortality or life expectancy rate, explicitly, of the youth or the children caused by the epidemic. Population of the orphaned children infected by the epidemic or health cost are well unrecorded.

The Picture

The designation of the 26th June, yearly, as the *International Day Against Drug Abuse and Illicit Trafficking* commemorating the *International Declaration Against Drug Abuse And Illicit Trafficking* on the 26th June, 1987, UN proclamation of the period 1991-2000 as *Decade against Drug Abuse* and the observation of the theme of the year just ended 2002 as the *Substance Abuse and HIV/AIDS* looked into the serious implications of drug abuse and illicit trafficking interwoven and the exposure of the youth to drug that brought the epidemic.

Manipur, a small landlocked state of the North-East India with hardly 0.2% of the country's population, by sharing a long stretch of 358 km with Myanmar on the east and the porous boundary intimately nestled on the *Golden Triangle* famous for 20% World heroin contribution precisely for production of high pure heroin type in crystal white injectable powder locally known as No. 4.

Of the two springs of narcotics, the golden Triangle in the South east Asia, a rugged mountainous terrain of about 2,000,000 sq.km with a population of approximately one million in around 3,000 villages comprising the Kachin Hills and the Shan plateau of Myanmar, the mountainous northern Laos and the northern hilly terrain of Thailand is one where heroin is manufactured in many laboratories controlled by various drug kings and trafficked to various destinations. Shan plateau and its neighbourhood (Myanmar); mountainous Chiang Mai, Chiang Rai, Mae Hongson and Nan province (Thailand); Hongsa and Louang Prabang province (Laos) are prominent poppy cultivation centres in the Golden Triangle.(The Golden Crescent on Afghan-Pak-Iran border is another one).

As per data available, the proximate corridors of drugs into the state are Tiddim and some other spots in the north-west Myanmar en-route Behiang, a Manipur-Myanmar border point in the Churachandpur district, far south Manipur touching the north-west Myanmar from where moved along the Imphal-Tiddim road connecting the capital town of Imphal and the Myanmar terminal point, Tiddim passing through Behiang and the proper Churachandpur town. Another well significant trafficking path since the early 80s into the state that reached the state capital, Imphal, via Moreh that found its way for filthy profitable export to Indian cities, Europe and United States. From being a transit in the trafficking, Manipur turned to be transit-consumer state characterised by the youth's entrance to drug addictive behaviour at a large proportion by the 80's and its consequential endemic in the society-the HIV/AIDS. Contrary to homosexual history of the epidemic in the United States, in Manipur, the genesis of the endemic is related to the high-risk addictive behaviour among the IDUS spreaded later by its own inherent multiplied potentiality. Interestingly, a huge percent of the HIV population is in the age range 15-35 years.

Table 8.1
Age-Sex Proportion of HIV Positive Cases (Sero-Surveillance)

Age Group	Male	Female	Total	% of Total Positives
11-20	847	293	1140	6.21
21-30	6067	2543	8610	46.88
31-40	4606	1638	6244	34.00

Source: Epidemiological Analysis of HIV/AIDS in Manipur upto August. 2006, Manipur State AIDS Control Society, Manipur.

Since the detection of the first HIV positive case in February 1990 from a cluster of IDUS blood samples collected in October 1989, HIV/AIDS has occupied a prime concern in the state. Prevalence rate among the IDUS increased from 0 to 50 % within a short span of one year during 1990-91. Manipur has earned the fame of contributing about 8% of the countries total HIV positive cases. Epidemiologically, Manipur ranks highest third in the HIV positive case after Maharashtra(first)and Tamil Nadu (second), albeit, calculation per one million population, Manipur's sero-prevalence rate is 6 times mightier than Maharashtra and 20 times that of Tamil Nadu.

Table 8.2
HIV/AIDS Sero-Sentinel Surveillance – Manipur

	Sero-surveillance	Sentinel-surveillance	Total
No. of blood samples screened	105284	50529	161813
No. of positives	18400	3490	21890
No. of Females	5323	—	5323
No. of AIDS cases	3831	—	3831
No. of deaths	549	—	549
Sero-positive rate per 1000 samples screened	174.44	97.12	147.43

Source: Epidemiological Analysis of HIV/AIDS in Manipur upto August 2006, Manipur State AIDS Control Society,Manipur.

Table 8.3
District-wise Break-up of HIV Positive Cases (Sero-Surveillance) – Manipur

District	No. of Samples Screened	HIV Positives	Sero-positivity Rate (%)	District %
Imphal	59970	11092	18.50	60.19
Thoubal	11955	1704	14.25	9.28
Bishnupur	7279	1070	14.70	5.83
Churachandpur	5631	1396	24.79	7.60
Ukhrul	3242	1094	33.74	5.96
Senapati	3634	787	21.66	4.29
Tamenglong	1088	68	6.25	0.37
Chandel	2558	795	31.08	4.33

Source : Epidemiological Analysis of HIV/AIDS in Manipur upto August 2006, Manipur State AIDS Control Society, Manipur.

Table 8.4
Sero–Positivity Rate and Percentage of the Intravenous Drug Users out of Total HIV Positives - Manipur

No. of Blood Samples Screened (Sero-surveillance)	No. of Positives (Sero-Surveillance	Sero-positive Rate of IDUs	% IDUs Out of Total HIV Positives
5284	18400	59.64	47.43

Source: Epidemiological Analysis of HIV/AIDS in Manipur upto August. 2006, Manipur State AIDS Control Society, Manipur.

Transmission Factors

The youth in their prime times are accessed to HIV/AIDS by a ray of transmission modes generally termed as 'immediate factor' that include unprotective-penetrative sex both heterosexual and homosexual, pre, during and post birth, parent to child transmission, transfusion transmission (blood products or blood sharing among the IDUs. Below, we may have a general table on sero-positivity among different high-risk groups under surveillance.

Table 8. 5
Sero-surveillance

High Risk Groups	Number Screened	Positive Number	Sero-positivity Rate
Heterosexual	20766	4767	22.96
Homosexual	140	36	25.71
Intravenous drug users (IDUS)	14607	8711	59.64
Antenatal Mothers	21979	412	1.87
Perinatal Transmission	2864	715	24.97

Source: Epidemiological Analysis of HIV/AIDS in Manipur upto August 2006, Manipur State AIDS Control Society, Manipur.

One point pertinent to be borne in mind is that while there has been some gains to reduce the high risk addictive behaviour among the IDUS, importance now herein lies into the perception and attitude of sexual behaviour otherwise the rate of transmission is triple the actual rate. This is what actually happened in the state where reduced high risk addictive behaviour is unreciprocated in terms of sexual behaviour increasingly transmitting to female spouses and children. But, what is of more relevance to the understanding of this epidemic is what could be designated as the 'underlying factor' which is 'structural' and 'environmental' in specific cultural context that encompass poverty, social and gender inequalities, population movements, human rights abuse societal denial and so on. The young people in the state are more prone to the endemic largely by the inappropriate education, dialogue on sex, sexuality and personal relations, lack of social support infrastructure embracing youth counseling and l health services, fluid political stability, high unemployment, absence of recreational facilities and usual violence confrontation made the youth to addictive behaviour. The vulnerability is more to the young women owing. It is further catalyzed by the older and sexually experienced men's preferential sexual tendency to younger women partnership, easier accessibility to money from the parents, family members and kin-network, influence of the drug addict peer group, temptation to taste, broken familial background, inappropriate parental care, frustration, unemployment, devoid of recreational accessibility and idea of a murky future . The situation is made a complex phenomenon by the easier availability of heroin, psychotropic substances and low cost locally brewing alcohol.

Connectivity

HIV/AIDS poses serious inter-knotted issues for social development. Like the twin transmission factor of the epidemic, there has, reciprocally, two implication types which constrained the development that may be distinguished for convenient analysis as 'immediate' and 'long term'. The immediate implication is squarely related to the effects brought about by the epidemic directly to the household and kin-line. Youth's utmost yearning to quench their addictive behaviour, extravagant treatment cost, on micro economic level drained a considerable chunk of long term aggregated household saving uninvested in productive purposes destabilizing the material well-being including household income, land and asset ownership, income stability et.al. Reduced aggregate saving and productive investment is natural outcome. The endemic caused slacked health status, absence of enterpreaunership enthusiasm and of household labour fastening familial impoverishment. HIV/AIDS is not just an individual concern; rather it is a social crisis by its character of potentiality to undermine the social fabric. Normality of growth is stressed by the epidemic. Within a short span of about one decade since its discovery in 1990,the epidemic dramatically metamorphosis the population profile in the state. Since its detection among the IDUS in 1990, HIV infection rate increases to 50% within six months. As the epidemic precisely strikes the active youth, a heightened mortality rate of this community of population is accounted that wives out a potential working force population leaving elderly and children at poles. The severity of the concern is the transmission of HIV infection from the IDUs to their non-injecting wives recording an increased percent from 6% (1991) to 45% (1997).While the increasing rate of pregnant mothers with HIV infection records from 1.3 (1994) to 2.7 (1999). The premature death of a promising section of the overall youth population erodes the infrastructure of human development of the state. Aside, the epidemic infected a considerable chunk of children. It heightened, considerably, the children being groomed under the single parenthood or orphaned by the death of both the parents or one. The situation of the orphaned children is quite acute by their vulnerability which is much more complex by the inappropriate extended familial and social support systems. In the long run, the endemic brought a demographic metamorphosis affecting human potential primarily due to enhanced youth's mortality in the productive time. In term of inter-generational consequences are clearly manifested by the sacrifice of long-term household security to meet the immediate needs finally in productivity-consumption slash. It, too, reduced the sectoral productivity.

The matter is more complex by its inherent dynamics of concealed build-up nature over time and costly intervention and programme implementation. Yet, effective timely commitment is necessity of the hours to save the future generation suffering the serious brunt of the epidemic towards social development orientation and to take care of the 'future risk of societal destabilization' by the formation of a 'poorly socialised and unskilled youth group.

Responses

1. Governmental Initiative:
2. Non-governmental Organisation's Initiative:
3. Civil Society Initiative:
4. Self Help Group Initiative:

A Thought

Since the past few decades, there have been initiatives taking care of the endemic; yet, there are gaps to the effective prevention strategies. This is an issue as such which is needed to be a sign a pragmatic-holistic response. Some of the primordial points that could perhaps be borne in mind towards social security:

— Creat conducive environment that could influence positive behaviour check. Social role to deliberate HIV/AIDS openly. Local, natinal and international actions to make enabling environt.

— Monitoring and Re-evaluation of the Harm reduction approach which is already in operation.

— Development of targeted information and accessibility to it via appropriat media for increasing awareness.

— Supportive services to enable to take steps to protect themselves including testing,conselling services, STD treatment programme.

— Sex and health education in school and peer education for out of school youths.

— Providing care and support to the infected and affected children and to identify and strengthen the traditional child support mechanism in the society.

— Prioritisation of issues by the governmental, non-governmental and general public support.

— Reviewing the existing the National and State AIDS policies. Need for culturally specific policy.

— Greater involvement of community towards sustenance for the effective intervention programme.

— Acknowledging HIV/AIDS not as a health issue rather a social concern within the larger context of development. It must not be considered as an isolated aspect of development.

REFERENCES

Dreze and Sen, *India : Economic Development and Social Opportunity*, Oxford University Press, 1995.

Das and Purkayastha (eds), *Border Trade: North-East India and Neighbouring Countries*, Akansha Publishing House, New Delhi.

Drug Situation and Demand Reduction Activities in Thailand, National Council on Social Welfare, Thailand, 1994.

Epidemiological Analysis of HIV/AIDS in Manipur up to August 2006.

Hirashima, *Social Sector of Economic Development: A Japanese Perspective*, Indian Social Science Review, Vol. 4, No. 1, Jan-June, 2002,

International Conference on Drug Abuse and Illicit Trafficking, Vienna, 17-26 June, 1987.

15th International Day Against Drug Abuse and illicit Trafficking (Joint publication,United nations Drug Control Programme, Manipur State AIDS Control Society,Social Welfare Department, Manipur and NGOs).

Political Declaration and Global Programme of Action,UN Decade Against Drug Abuse, 1991-2000.

Revisiting the hidden epidemic – a situation Assessment of drug use in Asia in the context of HIV/AIDS: India case, Centre for Harm Reduction, Australia, Jan. 2002.

Status Report Manipur (2004-05), Manipr State AIDS Control Society, Imphal, Manipur.

Sudhir, H. and Hajarimayum Jubita (eds), *Violence Against Women in North East India*, Akansha Publishing House, New Delhi, 2005.

Tarapot, *Drug Abuse and Illicit Trafficking in North Eastern India*, Vikas Publishing House, New Delhi, 1997.

9

OPIUM AND HEROIN PRODUCTION IN MYANMAR AND ITS IMPACT IN THE NEIGHBOURING COUNTRIES

—*L. Suresh*

Brief History of Opium

Opium is the name for the latex produced within the seed pods of the opium poppy, *Papaver somniferum*. The plant is believed to have evolved from a wild strain, *Papaver setigerum*, which grows in coastal areas of the mediterranean sea. Through centuries of cultivation and breeding for opium, the species somniferum evolved. Today, *P. somniferum* is the only species of *Papaver* used to produce opium. Opium contains morphine, codeine, noscapine, papaverine, and thebaine. All but thebaines are used clinically as analgesics to reduce pain without a loss of consciousness.

The psychological effects of opium may have been known to the ancient Sumerians (*circa* 4,000 B.C.) whose symbol for poppy wes hul, "joy" and gil, "plant". The plant was known in Europe at least 4,000 years ago as evidenced by fossil remains of poppy seed cake and poppy pods found in the Neolithic Swiss Lake Dwellings. Opium was probably consumed by the ancient Egyptians and was known to the Greeks as well. The word 'opium' is derived from the Greek. The poppy is referred to in

Homer's works the Iliad and the Odyssey (850 B.C.). Hippocrates (460-357 B.C.) prescribed drinking the juice of the white poppy mixed with the seed of nettle. The opium reached China about the fourth century A.D. through Arab traders.

In 1805, the German pharmacist Friedrich W. Sertyrner extracted and described the principal alkaloid and powerful active ingredient contained in opium. He named it *Orpheum* after *Orpheus*, the Greek god of dreams. We know it today as Morphine. The opium alkaloid Codeine was discovered in 1832 and palavering in 1848.

Opium was being heavily used in China as a recreational drug in the late 18th century. The Chinese Imperial court had banned its use and importation but large quantities were still being smuggled into China. In 1839 the Ding Emperor ordered his minister Lin Zexu to address the opium problem. Lin petitioned Queen Victoria for help but was ignored. The Emperor confiscated 20,000 barrels of opium and detained some foreign traders. In return the British retaliated by attacking the port city of Canton. Thus, the First Opium War began. The Chinese were defeated and the Treaty of Nanjing was signed in 1842. The British required that the Opium trade be allowed to continue, that the Chinese paid a large settlement, and that the Chinese ceded Hong Kong to the British Empire. The Second Opium War began and ended in 1856 over western demands that opium markets be expanded. The Chinese were again defeated and opium importation to China was legalized.

In the 1960s morphine was used extensively pre- and post-operatively as a pain-killer for wounded soldiers during the civil war. The inevitable result of opium addiction is called the 'army disease' or the 'soldier's disease'. These opium and morphine addiction problems promoted a scientific research for potent but non-addictive pain-killers.

In 1898 the Bayer Pharmaceutical Company of Germany was the first to make available this new drug, 3,6-

diacetylmorphine, in large quantities under the trade name Heroin. Heroin was initially used with much success as a superior cough suppressant for patients with tuberculosis. Tuberculosis patients continued to die, but without the tortuous coughing and pain. A second use of heroin was to combat morphine addiction - just as morphine was originally used to combat opium addiction. Soon after its introduction, however, Heroin was recognized as having narcotic and addictive properties far exceeding those of morphine*.

In December 1914, the United States Congress passed the Harrison Narcotics Act for control of each phase of the preparation and distribution of medicinal opium, morphine, heroin,cocain, and any new derivative that could be shown to have similar properties. It made illegal the possession of this controlled substance. In the mid-1970s Mexican brown heroin appeared.

The chemical structure of opiates is very similar to that of naturally produced compounds called 'endorphinsand enkephalins'. These compounds are derived from an amino acid pituitary hormone called 'beta-lipotropin' which when released is cleaved to form met-enkephalin, gamma-endorphin, and beta-endorphin, and beta-endorphin. Opiate molecules, due to their similar structure, engage many of the endorphin's nerve receptor sites in the brain's pleasure centers and bring about similar analgesic effects. In the human body, a pain stimulus usually exites an immediate protective reaction followed by the release of endorphins to relieve discomfort and reward the mental learning process. Opiates mimic high levels of endorphins to produce intense euphoria and a heightened state of well-being. Regular use results in increased tolerance and the need for greater quantities of the drug. Profound physical and psychological dependence results from regular use and rapid cessation bring about withdrawal sickness.

* Jim Hogshire, Opuim- poppy cultivation, morphine and Heroin manufacture.

In addition to the pleasure/pain centers, there is also a concentration of opiate receptors in the respiratory centre of the brain. Opiates have an inhibiting effect on these cells and in the case of an overdose, respiration can come to a complete halt. Opiate also inhibits sensitivity to the impulse to cough.

A third location for these receptors is in the brain's vomiting centre. Opiate causes nausea and vomiting. Tolerance for this effect is built up very quickly. Opiates affect the digestive system by inhibiting intestinal peristalsis. Long before they were used as pain-killers, opiates were used to control diarrhea.

The opium poppy, *Papaver somniferum*, is an annual plant. From a very small round seed, it grows, flowers, and bears fruits (seed pods) only once. The entire growth cycle for most varieties of this plant takes about 120 days.

The major legal opium poppy growing areas in the world today are in government-regulated opium farms in India, Turkey, Tasmania and Australia. The major illegal growing areas are in the highlands of Mainland Southeast Asia, specially Burma (Myanmar), Laos and Thailand, as well as the adjacent areas of southern China and northwestern Vietnam. The area is known as the "Golden Triangle". In the Southwest Asia, opium poppies are grown in Pakistan, Iran, and Afghanistan. Opium poppy is also grown in Lebanon, Guatemala, Colombia and Mexico.

The highlands of Mainland Southeast Asia, at elevations of 800 metres of more above sea level, are prime poppy growing areas. Generally speaking, these poppy-farming areas do not require irrigation, fertilizer, or insecticides for successful opium yields.

Most of the opium poppies of Southeast Asia are grown in Burma (Myanmar), specifically in the WA and Kokang areas, which are in the northeastern quadrant of the Shan State of Burma. Loas is the second-largest illicit opium-producing country in Southeast Asia and third largest in the world.

In Laos, poppy is cultivated extensively in Houaphan and Xiangkhoang provinces, as well as the six other northern provinces: Bokeo, Louangnamtha, Louangpghabang, Oudomxai, Phongsali and Xiagnabouli.

Morphine Extraction from Opium

Heroin manufacturers first extract the morphine from the opium before converting the morphine to heroin. The following is the step-by-step description of morphine extraction in a typical Southeast Asia laboratory:

1. An empty 55-gallon oil drum is placed on bricks about a foot above the ground and a fire is built under the drum. Thirty gallons of water are added to the drum and brought to a boil. Ten to Fifteen kilograms of raw opium are added to the boiling water.
2. With stirring, the raw opium eventually dissolves in the boiling water, while soil, leaves, twigs, and other non-soluble materials float in the solution. Most of these materials are scooped out of the clear brown 'liquid opium' solution.
3. Slaked lime (calcium hydroxide), or more often a readily available chemical fertilizer with a high content of lime, is added to the solution. The lime converts the water insoluble morphine into the water-soluble calcium morphenate. The other opium alkaloids do not react with the lime to form soluble calcium salts. Codeine is slightly water-soluble and gets carried over with the calcium morphenate in the liquid. For the most part, the other alkaloids become part of the residual sediment 'sludge' that comes to rest on the bottom of the oil drum.
4. As the solution cools, and after the insoluble precipitate out, the morphine solution is scooped from the drum and poured through a filter of some kind. Buriap rice sacks are often used as filters. They are later squeezed

in a press to remove most of the solution from the wet sacks. The solution is then poured into large cooking pots and re-heated, but not boiled.

5. Ammonium chloride is added to the heated calcium morphenate solution to adjust the alkalinity to a pH of 8 to 9, and the solution is then allowed to cool. Within one or two hours, the morphine base and the unextracted codeine base precipitate out of the solution and settle to the bottom of the cooking pot.
6. The solution is then poured off through cloth filters. Any solid morphine base chinks in the solution will remain on the cloth. The morphine base is removed from both the cooking pot and from the filter cloths; wrapped and squeezed in cloths, and then dried in the sun. When dry, the crude morphine base is a coffee-colored power.
7. This 'crude' morphine base, commonly known by the Chinese term *p'i-tzu* throughout Southeast Asia, may be further purified by dissolving it in hydrochloric acid, adding activated charcoal, re-heating and re-filtering. The solution is filtered several times, and the morphine (morphine hydrochloride) is then dried in the sun.
8. Morphine hydrochloride still stained with codeine hydrochloride is usually formed into small brick-sized blocks in a press and wrapped in paper or cloth. The most common block size is 2 inches by 4 inches by 5 inches weighing about 1.3 kg. The bricks are then dried for transport to heroin processing laboratories.

The conversion of morphine hydrochloride to heroin base is a relatively simple and inexpensive procedure. The necessary chemicals are readily available industrial chemicals. The equipment is very basic and quite portable. Heroin conversion laboratories are generally located in isolated, rural areas due to the tell tale odors of the lab's chemicals. Acetic anhydride, in particular, is a key chemical with the easily identify very pungent odour of pickles.

Heroin synthesis is a two-step process, which generally requires 12 to 14 hours to complete. Heroin base is the intermediate product. Typically, morphine hydrochloride bricks are pulverized and the dried powder is then placed in an enamel or stainless steel rice cooking pot. The liquid acetic anhydride is then added. The pot lid is tied or clamped on, with a damp towel used for a gasket. The pot is carefully heated for about two hours below boiling, at a constant temperature of 185°f. It is never allowed to boil or to become so hot as to vent fumes. Tilting and swirling until all the morphine have dissolved agitate it. Acetic anhydride reacts with the morphine to form diacetylmorphine (heroin). This acetylation process will work either with morphine hydrochloride or *p'i-tzu* (crude morphine based).

When cooking is completed, the pot is cooled and opened. The morphine and the acetic anhydride have now become chemically bonded, creating an impure form of diacetylmorphine (heroin). Water is added at three times the volume of acetid anhydride and the mixture is stirred. Activated charcoal is added and mixed by stirring and the mixture is then filtered to remove colored impurities. Solids remaining on the filter are discarded. Sodium carbonate, used at 2.5 pounds per pound of morphine, is dissolved in hot water and added slowly to the liquid until effervescence stops. This precipitates the heroin base which is then filtered and dried by heating in a steam bath for an hour,. For each pound of morphine, about 11 ounces of crude heroin base is formed. The heroin base may be dried, packed and transported to a heroin refining laboratory or it may be purified further and / or converted to heroin hydrochloride, a water-soluble salt form of heroin, at the same site.

Southeast Asian heroin base is an intermediate product which can be further converted to either a smoking form (heroin no. 3) or an injectable form (heroin no. 4)

Smoking Heroin, Heroin Hydrochloride

To make heroin no. 3 the crude base is mixed with hydrochloric acid resulting in heroin hydrochloride. Adulterants including caffeine are added after this conversion. For each kilogram of crude heroin about one kilogram of caffeine is used. Various 'flavourings' such as quinine hydrochloride or strychnine hydrochloride may be added in 7 gram or 14 gram increments. Next, the wet paste mix is stirred to dryness over the steam bath. The result-dry Heroin No. 3 will be in the form of coarse lumps. These are crushed and passed through a # 8 to #10 mesh sieve, and the grains (pieces) are then packaged for sale. The entire process takes about eight hours and requires only minimal skill. While extra attention to stirring is required to assure dryness, one man can prepare a one-kilogram block of Heroin No. 3 during this time.

Opium Production in Myanmar

Myanmar is one of the largest countries in Southeast Asia, with 676,552 sq. km with a population of 50 million. Almost half of the surface area is covered with forests and rugged hilly terrain. It has long borders with India, China, Thailand, as well as shorter borders with Bangladesh and Lao PDR. Myanmar ranked as the world's largest producer of opium accounting about 67% of the opium produced world-wide, and about 90% of that in Southeast Asia. The opium and heroin produced in the country are consumed in and distributed through China and Thailand as well as the rest of Asia, reaching destinations as far away as Australia, North America and Europe. Amphetamine Type Stimulants (ATS) produced in Myanmar, meanwhile, has fuelled drug-abuse of epidemic proportions in Thailand similar to that of Manipur. Addressing the drug problem in Myanmar is important not only for its international and regional ramifications, however, but also for the effects it has domestically at both the humanitarian and political levels. According to UNDCP in mid-2002 following the first ever comprehensive opium poppy survey for Myanmar, also indicated that the estimated 2002 production of about 828 metric tonnes of opium would be approximately 25% less than 1,097 tonnes produced in 2001. Between 1996 and 2002, production levels fell by just over 50%, from 1,760 to 828 tones, a sign of success for the increased control efforts on the part of the government and local authorities.

Despite the progress made in reduction of opium poppy cultivation, Myanmar also struggles with significant production of amphetamine type stimulants (ATS). The vast majority of opium and ATS production take place in the Shan state of northeastern Myanmar. The Shan state borders China, Laos and Thailand and forms part of the notorious Golden Triangle.

From 1996 to 2001, seizures of ATS tablets rose more than six-fold, from 5 million to 34.2 million tablets. Notably, ATS manufacturing in Myanmar is destined for export, implying a high level of cross-border complicity and lawlessness. Cross-border trafficking is an important characteristic of the drug trade in Myanmar, both for incoming precursor materials and outgoing illicit drug exports. The country has no chemical industry of importance. As such, most precursor chemicals required for the processing of drugs (refinement of opium and production of ATS) have to be imported. Both acetic anhydrides required for the production of heroin, and ephedrine required for production of ATS are imported from India and China.

Despite the large-scale illicit drug production and trafficking, the overall incidence of drug use in Myanmar is low compared to surrounding countries. The number of officially registered drugs in Myanmar reached 71,439 people in March 2001, although UNDCP estimates that up to 300,000 people might use illicit drugs. There is trend away from traditional opium smoking and towards the injection of heroin. This pattern has serious implications for the spread of HIV / AIDS, which is expanding in Myanmar at an alarming rate. After prostitution, injecting drug use is the main channel for HIV/AIDS transmission. Overall, 30% of officially reported HIV cases are attributed to injecting drug use.*

Myanmar shares a long and complex history with drugs. Hence, the issue has received attention from both the domestic and international. It is, however, not easy to deal with an intriguingly complex situation. For outsiders, it is often hard to understand where reality stops and friction starts. There is an impeding major crisis, which has and will further erode the civil society in Myanmar and has fuelled drug abuse of epidemic proportions in the North Eastern states of India and particularly in Manipur.

Drug Scenario of Manipur

This problem of drug abuse among the youths has assumed serious dimensions especially in the North Eastern and more particularly in Manipur. The proximity of the state towards the drugs producing region, "Golden Triangle" may be contributed to the cause of drug problem. In Manipur drug abuse problems have affected the Youths at thus most reproductive age of life.

Manipur besides its low socio- economic condition, suffers more problem of drug abuse especially heroin from early 1980's among the youths of Manipur irrespective of their background. The drug abuse problem affects the whole social strata of population. The state NGOs working in this field conservatively estimated about 15,000-20,000-heroin addict in the state in 1992. Although heroin addiction is decreasing due to cost factor and availability, Spasmoproxivon and other ATS are increasing in the late 90's and after 2000. The drug abuse pattern and

* United Nations response to HIV/AIDS in Myanmar –The United Nation Joint Plan of Action 2001-2002, UNSAIDS

their behaviors experienced in Manipur present a typical phenomenon and manifest unlike as elsewhere in the whole country. To study the situation we need to understand the entire gemmates of the socio-cultural background of the different community existing in state.

Profile of Drug Addiction and scenario by joint venture of the Divine light and Shine de-addiction centre, Imphal reflects the socio-economic and demographic status and pattern of drug abuse.

The study includes the initiation of drug use, mode of abuse, nature of drug abuse, duration of drug abuse, percentage of relapse and cause of drug abuse, district wise distribution etc. The study was based on 2375 males drug addicts admitted in the two de-addiction centre during mid 90's.

Socio-Economic and Demographic Profile

Districtwise distribution:

Imphal Distt.-3.70%, Bishnupur Distt-11.53%, Thoubal Distt.-18.14%, Churachandpur District-0.93%, Senapati Distt. -0.93%, Tamenglong Distt.-0.13%, others 2.11%. Here Churachandpur District shows very low percentage in spite of high numbers of Drug addict, this may be due to numbers of De-addiction centre in the district.

Age group:

Out of 2375 cases, 2093 addicts at the age group below 15 years shows low incident of 0.42% only, 16 years to 25 years shows second highest age group of 30.32%, 26 to 35 years - 55.58% the highest age group and 36 years and above shows Only13%. The highest is among the reproductive age group.

Religion:

The Meiteis Hindus were found to be the highest percentage of addiction of 88.13%, Muslims 6.86%, Christains - 4.13%.

Marital Status:

Unmarried - 70%, married - 25.94%, Divorced - 2.06%, Separate - 1.56%.

Education:

Secondary students were found to be the highest percentage; second and third comes to the graduate and higher secondary standard. This shows that educational attainments of these areas were surprisingly high among the literate group. This gives us the opportunity to implement any programme with less effort and successfully among these high literate groups. The research data shows that about 94% of drug addict attained above 10th standard.

In the national context illiterate group are more prone to addiction than the literate.

Family income:

Here, middle class group of Rs.2000 to 3000 monthly family income contributes the highest percentage that seeks drug addict's treatment. The income also reflects the type of addiction elsewhere but in Manipur the income is not must related to the type of addiction.

Referral services:

Family referral service shows 59.37% out of the 2375 drug addict admitted in the two centres, less in self, friend and other referral services. Most of the addicts want home detoxifications, which are not effective in most of the cases. The referral service is closely related to the income of the family, frequency of relapse, denial, fear, invulnerable attitude, stigma and social discrimination and lack of proper knowledge.

Mode of abuse:

About 93.01 percent of the admitted case in the study are Heroin (no.4) I.V. users which is the commonest in this state, only 5.64% of them chase drug. Recent trends shows SP IV user to be more common than the Heroin.

Nature of drug abuse:

The multi-drug using practice is more common in most of the drug abuse. In the study of the two centres, the multi-drug (heroin + others) contributes 80.13% against single (heroin) users of 8.25%.

The incidence of SP IV user is increasing day by day in this state and this indicates that the nature of drug abuse is changing during the last few years.

Period of drug abuse:

More than 70% used drugs for more than three years before seeking treatment.

Cause of Drug abuse:

Main cause of drug abuse in Manipur is due to peer group pressure; most of drug addicts hook onto drugs with their peers. This is the characteristic behaviors of the youths in the context of Manipur.

Recovery rate:

In most of the centre so far I have come across the high percentage of relapse case but in the data of the two centres the clean percentage is said to be 42.82% against the 22.40%.

REFERENCES

Global Illicit Drug Trends – 2002, ODCCP Studies on Drugs and Crime, UN Office for Drug Control and Crime Prevention.

International Narcotics Control Strategy Report – 2002, Bureau for International Narcotics and Law enforcement affairs, US states.

People's Power Against Drug addictive changes in South-East Asia, Harvard Asia Quaterly, September 2002.

ODCCP Country Profile: Myanmar 2001.

Strategic Programme Framework *UN Drug Control Activities in Myanmar*.

World Drug Report 2000, UN Office for Drug Control and Crime Prevention, Oxford University Press, 2000.

10

UNEMPLOYMENT IN MANIPUR: SOME POLICY IMPLICATIONS

—*Gurudas Das*
—*K. Gyanendra Singh*

As per 1991 census, Manipur shares 0.22 per cent of India's population. But as of 1997, the employment exchange statistics show that Manipur shares 0.81 percent of total live registered unemployed. These facts indicate the severity of unemployment problem in Manipur. As far as the northeastern region is concerned, the position of Manipur is next to Assam. While Assam shares 3 percent of the total live registered unemployeds, the same for Arunachal Pradesh, Meghalaya, Mizoram, Nagaland and Tripura is 0.03, 0.09, 0.17, 0.06 and 0.54 respectively (Table 10.1).

However, the data presented in table-10.1 shows only the tip of the iceberg. Besides the registrants on the live register, the number of non-registered unemployeds in urban areas and particularly their large presence in rural areas would certainly magnify the extent of unemployment problem in Manipur manifold. Once the underemployment dimension is added to it, the situation would seem to be explosive. Unfortunately, we do not classify information on the non-registered unemployeds as well as underemployed labour force.

However, if the tip of the iceberg is any indication of its size, then the number of registrants on the live register may be seen as symptomatic to explosive unemployment situation.

Table 10.1
All India Employment Exchanges statistics – State-wise 1997 (Figures in thousands)

State/Unoin Territory	Live Register	% of Live Register to Total Live Register
Andhra Pradesh	3087.5	7.89
Arunachal Pradesh	10.8	0.03
Assam	1475.0	3.77
Bihar	3351.3	8.56
Goa	109.0	0.28
Gujarat	942.3	2.41
Haryana	787.1	2.01
Himachal Pradesh	718.3	1.84
Jammu & Kashmir	164.7	0.42
Karnataka	1813.6	4.68
Kerala	3531.8	9.02
Madhya Pradesh	2377.4	6.07
Maharastra	3923.5	10.02
Manipur	318.1	0.81
Meghalaya	34.4	0.09
Mizoram	67.9	0.17
Nagaland	21.7	0.06
Orissa	977.3	2.50
Punjab	580.6	1.48
Rajasthan	873.8	2.23
Sikkim	—	—
Tamil Nadu	3896.1	9.95
Tripura	212.5	0.54
Uttar Pradesh	2696.8	6.89
West Bengal	5739.0	14.66

State/Unoin Territory	Live Register	% of Live Register to Total Live Register
A. & N. Islands	25.0	0.06
Chandigarh	124.7	0.32
D. & N. Haveli	5.5	0.01
Delhi	1097.4	2.80
Daman & Diu	5.5	0.01
Lakshadweep	8.8	0.02
Pondicherry	144.5	0.37
Total	**39139.9**	**100**

Source: Employment Exchange Statistics: 96-97, Directorate General of Employment and Training, Ministry of Labour, 1999.

Employment

Exchange data published by Manipur Government show another dimension of the severity of the unemployment problem in the state. Except for three years, the annual growth rate of the registrants on the live register during the period 1982-2003 has been positive and substantial (Table 10.2). For the three years for which negative annual rate has been observed, it is not because of the fact that in those years number of placements were very high. Rather, it appears that the negative growth rates were due to some other reasons like non-renewal of registration.

It is evident from Table 10.2 that for the period 1981-82 to 2002-03, the average annual growth of registrants on the live register stands at about 13718 persons. That is, every year during the reference period, it witnessed an additional 13718 persons registering themselves with the employment exchange. However, the average annual placement for the same period comes around 464 persons. This implies that it takes 29 years, assuming the present average annual rate of placement continues in future, to absorb the additional job seekers that appear in the job market in one year. Such being the case, what will happen to 28 generations?

Table 10.2
Registratoin And Placing Done Through Employment Exchanges In Manipur

Year	No. of registrants on the live register	Growth rate (%)	No. of persons placed in appointments	Total no. of placements (commulative figure)	Average annual change of no. of registrants	Average annual change of placements
1	2	3	4	5	6	7
1980-81	115546	—	703	703		
1982-83	153691	33.01	955	1658		
1983-84	176931	15.12	664	2322		
1984-85	194581	9.07	638	2960		
1985-86	237179	21.89	402	3362		
1986-87	266694	12.44	537	3899		
1987-88	249074	-6.61	1909	5808		
1988-89	248438	-0.26	226	6034		
1989-90	254310	2.36	292	6326		
1990-91	183495	-27.85	242	6568		
1991-92	198148	7.99	174	6742	13717.82	464.23
1992-93	215677	8.85	310	7052		
1993-94	241272	11.87	1390	8442		
1994-95	249910	3.58	1085	9527		
1995-96	276157	10.50	143	9670		
1996-97	299881	8.59	579	10249		
1997-98	322253	7.46	429	10678		
1998-99	354269	9.94	162	10840		
1999-2000	387890	9.49	69	10909		
2000-01	397304	2.43	2	10911		
2001-02	409652	3.11	—	10911		
2002-03	417338	1.88	5	10916		

Source: Statistical Handbooks of Manipur, *1992 and 2002.*

Assuming G1, G2, G3, . . ., G29 stand for first, second, third, . . ., twenty-ninth generations respectively, who are appearing in the job market in the first, second, third, . . ., twenty-ninth year given the average annual placement for the reference period, 464 persons will find job in the first year, another 464 in the second year, another 464 in the third year, and the last group has to wait for 28 years to get a job, if the placement is done on the first come first serve basis. If 29 years are needed to absorb G1, then persons in G2 will start getting jobs after 29 years. Assuming that they enter into the job market at the age of 16, then by the time the first batch of 464 from G2 is placed into job, they become 45 years old. Out of 29 batches in G2, when batch 13 comes in front of the queue, they attain retirement age of 58 and disqualify for getting any public assignment. Although this is a very simplistic way of looking at things, nonetheless, this thinking only reveals the horrible unemployment situation that is prevailing in Manipur. As most of the job seekers on the live register are educated youths, the scenario depicted above indeed portrays a very grim future for them.

It is only natural that this severe unemployment problem will lead to extreme frustration and anger. The present day socio-political instability in the state is intricately related with this problem of unemployment.

What is the way out, then? How can this problem be addressed? How can jobs be created for them? What are the options available to address this problem?

As the creation of jobs is linked with the growth of local economy and the solution of the problem ultimately lies with the issue of persistent economic growth, let us have a look at the structural change in the economy of Manipur.

II

NSDP data released by the Government of Manipur show a secular decline in the share of primary sector to total NSDP

(Table 10.3). The share of the primary sector was 48.74 per cent in 1980-81 and it has gone down to 38.36 percent in 1990-91, i.e., it has declined by about 10-percentage point in that decade. But in contrary, the share of main workforce engaged in primary sector remained constant (Table 10.4). This implies that the same workforce is now contributing less, i.e., the same workforce is now generating lesser income. It is evident from these facts that the rural sector is getting pauperized over the time.

Table 10.3
Revised Net State Domestic Product of Manipur at Constant 1980-81 Prices by Industry of Origin

Year	Primary Sector	Secondary Sector	Tertertiary Sector
1980-81	9792 (48.74%)	1663 (8.28%)	8635 (42.98%)
1981-82	10052 (47.33%)	1893 (8.91%)	9291 (43.76%)
1982-83	9821 (45.55%)	1927 (8.94%)	9812 (45.51%)
1983-84	10662 (45.39%)	2107 (8.97%)	10722 (45.64%)
1984-85	10906 (44.59%)	2308 (9.44%)	11243 (45.97%)
1985-86	11238 (43.43%)	2529 (9.77%)	12111 (46.80%)
1986-87	10959 (41.48%)	2542 (9.62%)	12917 (48.90%)
1987-88	11113 (39.70%)	2748 (9.82%)	14133 (50.48%)
1988-89	11300 (38.37%)	3045 (10.34%)	15105 (51.29%)
1989-90	11721 (38.11%)	3338 (10.85%)	15693 (51.04%)
1990-91	12659 (38.36%)	3725 (11.29%)	16615 (50.35%)

Source: Statistical Handbook of Manipur, 1992.

Table 10.4
Distribution of Working Population by Indusrtry

Industry	1971	1981	1991
Primary Sector	264421 (71.30%)	399033 (69.60%)	495792 (70%)
Secondary Sector	45361 (12.23%)	76568 (13.35%)	68404 (9.66%)
Tertiary Sector	61081 (16.47%)	97738 (17.05%)	144087 (20.34%)
Total Main Workers	370863	573339	708283
Total Population	1072753	1420953	1837149

Source: Census of India, 1971, Manipur, General Economic Tables, Series-12, Part II-B, Census of India, *1981, India, General Economic Tables, Series-1, Part II-A and Statistical Handbook of Manipur, 1992.*

As far as the secondary sector is concerned, its share in total NSDP has gone up from 8.28 percent in 1980-81 to 11.29 percent in 1990-91, i.e., an improvement little over 3 percentage point (Table 10.3). Here also contrary to this trend, the percentage of main workforce engaged in the secondary sector has declined from 13.35 percent in 1981 to 9.66 percent in 1991, i.e., a reverse change of more than 3 percentage point (Table 10.4). This implies that less number of people is now generating more income in the secondary sector. Whatever little growth has been registered in the secondary sector, it has negatively impacted upon the employment sector. A kind of jobless growth syndrome is observed in this case.

Coming to the tertiary sector, its share in NSDP also has registered some improvement. It has gone up from 42.98 percent in 1980-81 to 50 percent in 1990-01, i.e., an improvement little over 7 percentage point (Table 10.3). Only in this sector, we observe that some additional jobs have been created. The percentage of main workforce engaged in this sector has gone up from 17.05 percent in 1981 to 20.34 percent in 1991, i.e., a growth of about 3-percentage point (Table 10.4). It may be noted that even in the tertiary sector, the rate at which its share has increased in NSDP is more than double the rate at which it has absorbed the additional workforce.

III

The above analysis brings to the fore the stagnant nature of the economy of Manipur. Given the severity of the unemployment problem, there is no other way than to dynamise the economy. As the educated job seekers are unlikely to seek jobs in the primary sector, the focus should be on the secondary and tertiary sectors. As far as the secondary sector is concerned, a strong dyadic linkage needs to be established between the local resource base and local industrial structure. Once the resource-industry linkage is strengthened, then it will have bearing on both the primary and tertiary sectors. Without the organic linkage among the three sectors, none of them could grow persistently. The vibrancy of the economic system depends primarily on the role of the secondary sector. Hence, the primary focus should be on the strategy as to how to strengthen the secondary sector.

Given the fact that due to political instability / insurgent activity, private investment in the secondary sector is hard to realize, the public sector has to play the major role in boosting up the secondary sector. Again, given the fact that public sector is subject to corruption, inefficiency, nepotism, political interference, it is unlikely that the existing pattern of public sector initiative will work. Here lies the need to evoke an alternative policy for government intervention. Public sector initiatives, instead of routing through bureaucratic structure, may be launched in association with community-based organization. The financial resources mobilized by the government may be invested for the creation of industrial capacities and then the asset created in the process may be handed over to community based organization for management. Income generated in the process may be shared between government and the community. This will, on the one hand, empower the community economically and on the other ensure the sustainability of the industrial unit.

The ideas expressed here are tentative and germinating. They need to be developed further and enriched.

11

ENTREPRENEURSHIP EDUCATION AND TRAINING: IT'S ROLE IN SOLVING UNEMPLOYMENT PROBLEMS IN MANIPUR

—G.P. Prasain

Abstract

Manipur literally name "A Jewelled Land" is located in the extreme northeastern corner of India with a population of 23,88,634 and out of this 4,34,488 are unemployed who have registered their name in the various Employment Exchange of Manipur. Among these registered unemployed, 1295 are engineering graduates, 350 are computer graduates and 450 are agricultural graduates. Apart from this there are many unemployed persons who have not registered their names in the employment exchanges. One of the important reasons for having a large name of educated unemployed youth in the state of Manipur is lack of proper education and training which help them in becoming self employed. Therefore we need entrepreneurial education and training that will develop self-confidence among the educated people and train them to start their own industry and ultimately they may become job givers and not job seekers.

Entrepreneurship development has been accepted in our country as a strategy for achieving the twin objectives of solving the problem of unemployment, particularly among the educated unemployed youth and also for rapid industrialization. It was started during the early sixties in the form of industrial campaign. It has taken the form of a countryside movement. Entrepreneurship among the youth has become vital for the following reason.

1. *The Government cannot provide all types of jobs for all types of unemployed youth.*
2. *The private sector will provide jobs to the best but there is no job security.*
3. *Jobs may be available outside the state of Manipur but many people of Manipur cannot move out due to various reasons.*
4. *The ideal job is never found.*
5. *A job will provide income for one family but an entrepreneurial venture will support more than one family.*

This is how entrepreneurship education and training comes in the picture. It has to act as the bridge to gap the span between the dreamers and doers. If a proper bridge can be built then we can see a host of entrepreneurial activity in our state. The bridge i.e. entrepreneurship education has to be made popular as far as possible. Depending on the qualifications, exposure and level of self-confidence different training modules will have to be designed not only for the potential entrepreneurs but also for the personnel in the support organizations, which will ultimately help in solving unemployment problems in the state of Manipur.

Introduction

The size of employment in any country depends considerably on the level of development. Therefore, when a country makes progress and its production expands, the employment opportunities often grow. In India, during the past three decades or so production has expanded in all the sectors of the economy. In response to these developments the absolute level of employment has also grown. However, during the planning period, unemployment in absolute term has increased. This has happened because during the planning period trend rate of growth was considerably lower than the targeted rate. Therefore, jobs in adequate number were not created. Further, economic growth by itself does not solve the problem of unemployment. The possibility of an increase in unemployment is not to be completely out in a rapidly developing economy.

Employment in Organized and Unorganized Sectors

The India economy is divided into organized and unorganized sectors. The unorganized sector in this country is quite large. Whole of agriculture is in the unorganized sector. Besides agriculture, most of mining, manufacturing, construction, trade, transport and communication, social and personal services are in the unorganized sector. Organized sector by and large is restricted to manufacturing, electricity, transport and financial services. Organized sector employment in 1999-2000 was 28.11 million i.e., about 7.08% of the total employment of about 397 million. Interestingly, despite economic reforms employment in the organized sector has been declining in percentage terms. The unorganized sector accounts for less than half of the GDP and it provides employment at around 93% of the labour force.

Nature of Unemployment

Most of the unemployment in India is definitely structural. During the 1961-2001 period, population in this country had grown at an alarming rate of around 2.15 percent per annum and with it the number of people coming to the labour market in search of jobs had also increased rapidly, whereas employment opportunities did not increase most of the time correspondingly due to slow economic growth. Hence, there has been an increase in the volume of unemployment from one plan period to another. Apart from structural employment there is same cyclical unemployment, which has emerged mainly in urban areas as a result of industrial recession. For analytical convenience the unemployment in India is classified as (i) urban unemployment and rural unemployment. Urban unemployment is mainly of two types (a) industrial unemployment (b) educated unemployment. Rural unemployment is classified as (a) open unemployment and (b) disguised unemployment. A special type of open unemployment in the countryside known as seasonal unemployment is of considerable importance in the Indian economy.

Causes of Unemployment

The main causes of unemployment in India are as follows:

(i) *Jobless Growth*

Economic growth is usually expected to generate employment. However, in India most of the time growth has been jobless. For 30 years from 1950-51 to 1980-81, GDP growth rate was as low as 3.6 per annum. At this rate of economic growth many jobs could not be created. GDP growth accelerated to 5.6 per annum in the 1980s and stayed at this level in the 1990s. At this higher rate of GDP growth one would normally expect that many new employment opportunities would be forthcoming. But this could not happen in India. During the last two decades there was a steep decline in employment elasticity in almost all the major sectors.

(ii) *Increase in Labour Force*

In India death rate has rapidly decline since independence, and the country has entered the second stage of demographic transition. The rate of population growth rate to 2.2% per annum during the 1960s, and as a consequence, rate of increase in labour force also rose to 1.9 per cent per annum. During the last three decades both demographic and social factors have further raised the rate of growth of labour force. Over the years mortality rate has declined rapidly without a corresponding fall in birth rate and the country has thus registered an unprecedented population growth,. This was naturally followed by an equally large expansion of labour force. In Indian context, social factors, affecting the labour force are as much important as demographic factors. Since independence, education among women has changed their attitude towards employment. Many of them now compete with men for jobs in the labour market. The economy has, however, failed to respond to these challenges and the net result is continuous increase in unemployment backlog. In rural areas, whereas an account of growing labour force unemployment has increased mainly in disguised form, in urban areas it is open and visible.

(iii) *Inappropriate Technology*

In India while capital is a scarce factor, labour is available in abundant quantity. Under these circumstances, if market force operates freely and efficiently, the country would have labour intensive techniques of production. However, not only in industries, but also in agriculture producers are increasingly substituting capital for machine and other sophisticated equipment is both rational and justified while in India, on account of abundance of labour, this policy results in large unemployment. When labour force is in excess supply at prevailing monetary rates of return, capital would not be considered productive, if it does the same work which labour also does with an equal amount of efficiency. Investment in such a situation in capital equipment may be profitable ti individual capitalists, but it is certainly not beneficial to the society, but it increases unemployment and not production.

Inappropriate Education System

The prevailing educational system, which is being followed in India, is defective. It is, intact, the same educational system which Macauley had introduced during the colonial period. According to Gunnar Myrdal, India's educational policy does not aim at development of human resources. It may merely produce clerks and lower cadre executive for the government and private concern. With the expansion in the number of institution, which imparts this kind of education, increase in unemployment is inevitable. It is so because arts, commerce and science will not ensure employment on account of its limited utility for productive purposes. Myrdal considers all those who receive merely this kind of education not only as inadequately educated but also wrongly educated. Myrdal's criticism of India's educational system is valid. If the problem of unemployment is to be solved in the country, radical changes will have to be made in it. Any educational system which fails to develop human resources properly will not be able to provide employment to all those who have received it and hence has to be changed to make it employment oriented.

Keeping in view the drawbacks of present education system, which has failed to produce human resource capable of becoming self employed, an attempt has been made in this paper to study and suggest a proper education system which will help in solving unemployment problem in India as well as in Manipur.

Unemployment Problems in Manipur

Manipur is located in the extreme northeastern corner of India between 23.80 N to 25.68 N latitude and 93.03 E to 94.78E longitude and occupies a total area of 22, 327 sq. km. Of its total area, about nine-tenth constitute the hills which surround the remaining central valley of alluvial filling. It is bounded by Nagaland in the north, Assam on the west and Mizoram on the south. Along the east it shares a 352 km. long international boundary with Mynmar. Manipur has a population of 23,88,634 and out of this male population is 12,07,388 and female population is 11,81,29. The rural and urban population of Manipur is 18,18,224 and5, 70,410 respectively with a sex ratio of 978 female per 1000 male and the literate population of Manipur is 14,29,656 which constitute about the 68.87% of the total population. The figures of the jobseekers who have registered their names in the various employment exchanges of Manipur is 4,34,488 which is very high and it is 18.20% of the total population of the state. In addition to these there are many people who have not registered their names formally in the employment exchanges. There is seasonal and disguised employment in agricultural sector also. Thus, the unemployment situation is very alarming in the state of Manipur. One of the reasons for deteriorating law and order situation, growing social tension and up rise of continuing emphasis on liberal education has only swelled the number of unemployment, promote unrest among students. Distort planned strategies of development and tend to part the economy of Manipur towards a state of chaos. Again, job opportunities has become limited, hence, there is the greater need for chanalizing the resurgency and potentialities of youth of our state in constructive direction. Therefore, there is a strong need to change the present education system to make our educated youth self employed and to develop the state's economy and this can be achieved by introducing entrepreneurship and training in course curriculum of colleges and universities.

Demerits of Present Education System

Younger generation feels frustrated because they do not have assurance that their education and scientific talents would be fully utilized. Our education system has produced huge number of educated unemployed youths. Our college and university education itself is perhaps not enough to prepare students to take up entrepreneurial as career. This happens because of the following demerits found in the present education system.

1. Students acquire theoretical knowledge of the subjects they study, but they lack skills to use their knowledge in practice. There is lack of practical exposure both to the teachers and the students. Subjects are theoretically taught at the classroom without practical exposure.
2. Present-day do not know about the various

opportunities for self-employment as they are not made aware during the course of their study.

3. Students believe that they would get a job when they complete their study that actually does not happen, and they have to struggle a lot to get a job.
4. Parents also generally do not encourage their children to take up entrepreneurship as career. They want their sons and daughters to do white collared jobs because of assured income, less risk, lesser hours of hard work and less degree of responsibility.
5. People's mindset in our society gives higher status to a salaried person than self employed entrepreneurs.
6. Students are not motivated to take up entrepreneurship as a career. They are not aware of the various opportunities, which exist in the market.
7. The role of promotional agencies, financial institutions and development organization is not satisfactory as they seldom take up awareness programme among the community, more particularly students on entrepreneurship.

Therefore, we can say that the environment in the family, society, educational institutions and the support system in the organizational level are generally not conducive to encourage the students to consider entrepreneurial ship career as an option. It is, therefore, necessary to take up various measures for converting the job givers into job seekers through entrepreneurialship education and training.

Unemployment and Entrepreneurship

In industrial developed of a country is considered to be an engine of growth to accelerate its overall economic development. Industrial development cannot, however, progress without development of entrepreneurship. In fact, promotion and development of small industries considered vital for ameliorating the scourge of unemployment with less capital investment is intimately linked with development of entrepreneurship. Moreover, the phenomenon of over growing unemployment especially among the educated youth in Manipur seems to warrant induction of the long felt need based skills that improve the employability leading to self employment. Unemployment amongst the educated young men and women in Manipur is one of the disturbing signs of weakness of state economy. It is all more distressing to see young qualified professionals in the state not gainfully employed. Since the economic growth and unemployment are mutually incompatible this imbalance must be stalled by stimulation of a spectacular growth of small industry based on local resources and skill. In this context the concept of human resource development has also become very much relevant. Human resources development in broad sense means organized learning and living experience, which is goal, directed towards progressive transformation of society in social and economic terms. It means making human strength more productive and more egalitarian. It implies a strategy of development that is adequately needful of individual and social concerns.

Entrepreneurship and Education

As we have experienced that the trend of education in developing countries like India, the emphasis is generally laid on producing graduates fit only for job without any motivation and competence for entrepreneurial capabilities. By and large, the developing countries have uncritically adopted the traditional pattern of education of advanced countries where in sharp contrast to developing countries job opportunities exist and are expanding. The basic attitudes of our institutions also emanates from this historical context. The developing countries in the colonial times were so to say administrative states. The government monopoly produced corresponding attitude of widespread abject reliance on it for the generation of activity. This attitude was abetted by certain social traditions of the societies, which also contributed to inhibiting individual capacity of adventure. The net results have been that while these societies offer wide scope to enterprising professionals in actual practice one witnesses massive unemployment. The graduates that our educational institutions are producing are looking for certain niches in the society, which do not exist whereas tremendous opportunities exist for entrepreneurial opportunities. It follows that our education should provide opportunity and promotes development of entrepreneurial attitudes and capabilities. Therefore, a change in the present education system towards entrepreneurship oriented is highly desirable.

Reorientation of Education

As mentioned, the state is facing acute problem of unemployment, particularly of educated unemployed. In spite of all the development that has taken place apparently there is an insufficiency of salaried jobs to absorb all the educated people who have come out from the colleges and universities. Considering the large sum of money spent in the education and training of a single graduate, may be in any discipline or subjects, the fact that so many of them are not gainfully employed means colossal waste of our meager resources. Obviously it would be better if during the course of study in college and university emphasis is given for proper motivation for self-employment in addition giving the minimum procedural know how necessary for starting a venture for self-employment. There is an imperative need for creating among our students a new climate of preference of self-employment and entrepreneurial activity. The education must be given a new orientation so that our young graduates will have the skills, incentives and facilities to go for self-employed enterprises. An educational institution cannot survive without involvement in the problem of life and without learning through it. Hence, the following measures may be suggested to develop entrepreneurial attitudes among the students:

1. First of all, it is necessary to create an enterprising environment in the economy as well as entrepreneurial attitudes among the unemployed youth and students. For this, the youngster should be connected intimately with the business. The very trend of the middle class ideology has to be reshaped by completing and even substituting, if necessary, the belief of traditional education to that of professional education, human moral code to a strong set of business ethics and the idea of a steady job to risk taking for better earnings. All these require extensive moral boosting and confidence building efforts on the part of the Government, academic and professional institutions and the NGOs.

2. Entrepreneurship education has to be customized as far as possible. Depending on qualifications, exposure and level of self-confidence, different training modules will have to be designed for the students of various classes.

3. Considering the need of the time, educational institutions should form a separate cell to encourage and guide their students towards entrepreneurship development in the line of their technical and/ or professional knowledge and expertise.

4. Various academic body and universities should develop the curriculum according to the need of the society more specifically that of the market, and integrating them with various state-sponsored schemes introduced for self-employment generation and entrepreneurship development.

5. A module on entrepreneurship development should be an integral part of syllabus to make the students aware of various aspects of entrepreneurship development and motivate them in this direction.

6. It is observed that many of the enterprising efforts, particularly the small and tiny ones, fail because of the lack of necessary entrepreneurial and managerial competencies on the part of entrepreneurs. Not only that in today's extensively competitive business environment traditional entrepreneurial and managerial knowledge and skills need to be attuned to the new environment and systems on regular basis. Therefore, to make students familiar with entrepreneurial culture, seminar, conference, workshops, training programme and awareness programme should be organized on regular basis with the professionals and experts from the relevant fields as resource persons to guide the students.
7. Decision to be an entrepreneur may, to a large extent, be influenced by the financial performance and growth prospects of the existing enterprises. While healthy financial performance of the existing enterprises may not necessarily encourage the unemployed youths to start their own venture, sickness in these concerns can surely demotivate them in their efforts. Therefore, the Government should provide necessary technical and managerial support to the existing small and tiny enterprises, particularly, the sick ones to improve their financial performance and thereby, to encourage the educated unemployed youth to enter into the business in the present era of liberalization, privatization and globalization.

Conclusion

To secure employment to the unemployed, particularly to the educated ones, has now been the thrust of all economic development activities. In the special circumstances prevailing in Manipur, unemployment has been the cause for a number of other problems and therefore, tackling of it has assumed great importance. Entrepreneurship development has been accepted in our country as a strategy for achieving the twin objectives of solving problems of unemployment, particularly among the educated unemployed youth and also for rapid industrialization. Wide-scale development of entrepreneurship can help not only in generating self-employment opportunities and, thereby, reducing unrest and social tensions amongst the unemployed youths but also in introducing small business dynamism, encouraging innovative activities and facilitating the process of balanced economic development,

REFERENCES

Desai, Vasant, *Entrepreneurship and Small Bussiness Management*, Himalaya Publishing House, Mumbai, 2000.

Journal of the North Eastern Council, North-Eastern Council, Shillong

Khamka, S.S., *Entrepreneurial Development*, S. Chand & Co., New Delhi, 2002.

Kangleipak Business Review, Department of Commerce, Manipur University, Imphal.

Mali, D.D., *Entrepreneurship Development in North East*, Indian Institute of Entrepreneurship, Guwahati, 2000.

Prasain, G.P., *Entrepreneurship Development*, Sunmarg Publishers and Distributors, New Delhi, 2003.

Puri and Mishra , *Indian Economy*, Himalaya Publishing House, New Delhi, 2002.

Rao, J.V. Prabhakara, *Entrepreneurship and Economic Development*, Kanishka Publishers and Distributors, New Delhi, 2000.

Statistical Hand Book of Manipur, Directorate of Economics and Statistics, Government of Manipur, 2001.

Yojana, Ministry of Information and Broadcasting, Government of India, New Delhi.

12

EMPLOYMENT OPPORTUNITIES IN NORTH-EAST INDIA

—Indraneel Bhowmik

Abstract

Economic backwardness and insurgency are the two major concerns for the North East India. "Whether unrest and insurgency have kept the region backward or persistence of backwardness has fermented and sustained unrest is also endlessly debated". Moving away from the debate, we can say the people at large is being affected and an entire generation, the present day youth, is going ashtray.

No doubt the social conflicts arising from transition process with communities and ethnic groups as external and exogenous factors have played their dubious role to enhance the crisis, but the economic component remains no less important.

This paper stems to look at the development perspective from the economic point of view. The present paper attempts to identify the problems faced by youths of the region and further endeavours to suggest remedies at both micro and macro level. Titled as "A ride to vocation" the study uses secondary data available from different sources and also draws inferences from primary experiences gathered on various field trips as a social scientist. The methodology adopted for this paper would include standard econometric application through the use of standard statistical tools.

Section I

Fault lines along ethnic, linguistic, racial, cultural and religious dimensions characterize the seven states; yet, in most cases we refer to this region of India as the Northeast. Though politically incorporated in the Indian union at different stages, these states share the commonality of economic backwardness and insurgent crossfire. Well "whether unrest and insurgency have kept the region backward or persistence of backwardness has fermented and sustained unrest .... (Bezbaruah, 2004) is not our topic; the grim reality is both exist. Northeast India today is synonymous with daily events of extortions, kidnapping, shooting, killing as well as large scale ethnic clashes creating wide spread fear psychosis among the people of the region as well outside. Though several exogenous and external factors exist, the inter-linkage between economic backwardness and insurgency appears relatively stronger. Limited opportunities to youth for earning a livelihood often causes derailment and the brunt of the mislead energy is felt on the society.

Corruption, unemployment and poverty are the malaise that plague India today and hinders the country's developmental march to progress. Situation in Northeast is not different. The present paper attempts to study on one of these major slumps- the unemployment situation in the region. The paper has been organized in five sections including this introduction. Section II reviews the performance of the region in terms of its macroeconomic parameters. The third section is an attempt to understand the employment-unemployment scenario of the region and is followed by another section identifying the potential employment opportunities in the region. The final section sums up the paper and endeavours to suggest certain policy initiatives.

Section II

The North-Eastern states home to almost 4 crore Indians

exhibit the common features of a less developed economy. Agriculture is the dominant sector in the region followed by limited secondary and tertiary sectors. The region's share in the country's NNP is 33.5%. But unlike India's current sectoral composition, the share of both manufacturing/industrial and service sector in the North East is much limited. However, agriculture though predominates, in most cases the traditional way is practised where technological applications are low. The average yield of food-grains in Northeast is much lower than the national average. Even the compound annual growth rate (CAGR) for productivity in this region has been 1.17% only. Assam owing to its inherent advantage of the perennial water facilities of the Brahmaputra and, its tributaries has the largest acreage but the crop returns are much better in Manipur and Tripura. Manipur should be proud for its achievements in rice cultivation. It is to be noted here that Mizoram the post reform phase has been performing steadily in respect to yield food grains.

Table 12.1

Sectoral Composition of the NE States (%) 2000-01

States	Primary	Secondary	Tertiary
Arunachal	35.42	31.04	33.54
Assam	47.69	14.74	37.57
Manipur	38.96	9.84	51.20
Meghalaya	30.79	14.40	54.81
Mizoram	37.14	14.68	48.18
Nagaland	32.21	10.11	57.68
Tripura	43.27	6.62	50.11

Source: Calculated from several issues of *Economic Survey and NEDFI databank,www.northeast. nic.in*

Table 12.2
Progress of Agriculture: Yield of foodgrains (kg/ha in the Northeast)

State	1986-87	1991-92	1996-97
Arunachal	1069	1165	1176
Assam	1003	1229	1294
Manipur	1491	2131	2265
Meghalaya	946	1163	1141
Mizoram	1002	1367	1726
Nagaland	633	1116	1062
Tripura	1308	1786	2039
Northeast	1037	1300	1378
All India	1128	1382	1601

Source: Calculated from CMIE Agricultural Data, NEDFI databank, www.northeast. nic.in

The country's oldest oil well is in Northeast but unfortunately the industrial developments of the region have been limited. Tea as an industry is a major contributor to the economy both in terms of employment and revenue generation and has been the basis for Assam's developments from the last quarter of the 19th century. Several ancillary industries like plywood, coal, railway sleepers, etc. had developed. The traditional weaving and handicrafts sector has been a major contributor to the local economy from time immemorial. Bamboo and cane products of this region have a very good domestic and external market. However, the development of consumer goods industry or heavy industries in this region has been always limited following several factors. Modern technological progress has been incorporated in the past few decades through setting up of paper mills. Availability of raw material is a major cause behind such steps. However, among the seven states heavy and medium scale industries are more prominent in Assam and Meghalaya only.

The services sector in the Northeast is no doubt dominant in terms of its share in NSDP, and its share is more or less in parity to the national level statistics. This sector however gains strength owing to the expanding public administration and other services. Performance of this sector has immense contribution from the educational sector. The number of educational institutes catering to the needs of the sector is almost 67,000 in members. However, this figure includes all categories of institutes ranging from pre-primary section to universities. The institute student ratio in the Northeast India has been much higher than the rest of the country and has been evidenced through much higher literacy rates in the region.

Table 12.3
Land Utilization in North East Region (1995-96)

Character of Land use	NER (%)	All India (%)
Forest Land	52.38	22.57
Not available for cultivation	19.61	13.58
Uncultivable land	7.00	9.40
Fallow land	3.63	7.81
Net area sown	17.38	46.64

Source: NEDFI databank, ***www.northeast.nic.in***

The economy of the Northeast India is predominantly agricultural as is evident in Table 12.1. The process of industrialization has been slow mainly due to locational disadvantages and indifferent attitude of the central Government in the heydays of government regulation. Yet industrial growth is not that happening in the post-liberalized phase. Tripura, smallest in size has the lowest degree of industrialization, as the only two medium sized industry - Tripura jute Mill and NERAMAC are forth closed. Revival packages have not been successful. Non-economic factors that loom large are today's industrial investment decisions. One cannot ignore the several fiscal incentives yet investments have been less than expected levels. The per capita NSDP at current price of North Eastern states is lower than India's per capita income in the post reform period (Bezbaruah, 2004). Persistence of high growth rates of population has dragged the economic performance of the three crore populous states Assam, Tripura and Meghalaya.

Section III

Unemployment Scenario

The major concern of the country today is no doubt the precarious unemployment scenario. The policy initiatives undertaken at the national level have not sufficed to the core. Theoretical explanations on unemployment as per Keynesian analysis consider the lack of effective demand as the cause. But the situation in India is different. It is more a cause of shortage of capital equipment or other complementary resources. Added to the woe is the ever-increasing population. The high growth rate of population in the 1970s and 80s have resulted in an increased number of unemployed youths nowadays. Moreover the structural adjustment programme as per the economic reforms has changed the country's approach to employment. Public sector, set up to serve the social welfare goal of the nation, plays a much lesser role. Employment generation or provision has been a major objective of the sector; naturally shrinkage of the public sector has reduced the intake of new workforce into its fold.

The North-east has experienced wide spread influx owing to partition. The land-man ratio in Assam and Tripura has increased manifold, whereas economic opportunities has not been commensurate with population increase. The sectoral employment for both the North East and the country as a whole has been the highest in Agriculture, followed by tertiary and industrial sector.

It is to be noted that absence of strong secondary sector or manufacturing sector in particular has created an immense pressure on agriculture in the North East. State Governments have a major employer especially for white-collar jobs. Lack of large industrial units has also limited the growth of the organized sector. The plantation sector- tea in Assam has a sizeable working population but the recession in tea trade has resulted in closures of many gardens.

Education

The education sector in India has made rapid progress. Literacy levels have risen though large number of Indians is still bereft of the fortune of reading and writing. However, expansion of education has swelled the number of educated unemployed. Size of educated unemployment remains largely unmeasured. Not only there are conceptual difficulties in estimating it, but also the kind of statistical information required for its estimation is also not available. Hence, the quantitative base for analyzing the problem of educated unemployment is weak. Table-12.4 provides the scenario of the educated unemployed in Tripura. Though it is not necessary that whoever has registered in the employment exchange is an unemployed. But there are several others who feel that registering himself/herself in the exchange is a fruitless effort. Most of tile students who out-migrate to the main land for perusing higher education do not come back to the region for their service life. There are limited opportunities in the region as well as the lure of higher levels of living.

Education in India has in most cases been a Government initiative. The State Universities outnumber the private universities. The later, mostly cater to technical and management educations and owing to their inherent business attitude has been more effective in providing or rather preparing their students for the job market.

Table 12. 4
Number of unemployed registered with the Employment exchange of the Government of Tripura

Category	Number
Madhyamik (School Final)	85971
Higher Secondary	23405
Graduates	34556
Post graduates	4933
Engineer (Bachelor Degree)	629
Engineer (Master Degree)	05
Engineer (Diploma)	819
ITI	3098
MBBS	141
B Sc (Agri)	423
M.Sc (Agri)	42
Law Graduates	33
Less than Class VIII	66629
Less than Class VII	66629
Less than Madhyamik	170540
Skilled & Semi skilled	10494
Others	5587
Total	**407005**

Source: The Chief Minister's reply to the Bidhan Sabha, Dainik Sambad, June 18 2004.

In order to find a way out for the growing number of unemployed, the Government of India had set up a Taskforce on Employment Opportunities under the stewardship of Prof. Montek Singh Ahluwalia, Deputy Chairman, Planning Commission, with the goal for providing jobs to ten crore people for ten years.

Table 12.5
Additional Employment created

	1983-93	Post reform
Primary	51%	–23%
Secondary	19%	50%
Tertiary	30%	73%

Source: Planning Commission, 2001

It is obvious that post-reform phase experienced higher growth rates in Secondary and tertiary sector as has been identified in the data available.

Agriculture

That agriculture has very limited opportunities is also evident in table 13.6. It is the tertiary sector that has the highest potential for job creation. Also to be noted is the prospect of the construction sector. The second generation economic reforms which are inherent in the plans and policies reflect the domination of the new generation industries which are know'ledge based, capital intensive and hugely competitive.

Section IV

Geography of NER

Northeast India has its distinct serenity and beauty of its own, rich with forests, flora and fauna, perennial rivers with the mighty Brahmaputra and its tributaries as a continuous source of energy. Endowed with natural beauty, simple and unassuming human resource this region has all it requires to be developed yet the Northeast remains the most backward region of the country. Unemployment, which is often, the cause cited for the derailment of the youths can be solved provided honest efforts are undertaken.

Geographically the Northeast has a chicken neck corridor with the rest of India through North Bengal. Actually 98% of the region's parameter has an international neighbour, namely- Bangladesh, Bhutan, China and Myanmar. Tripura the tiniest state of the region is encircled by Bangladesh over about 80% of her border. Interesting is the fact that though we have only about 8% of the country's area and 3% of the countrymen, 33% of the country's total international border lies in the northeast India. Obvious to any sane person, that the huge extent of international border facilitates influx of foreigners into the region. But the even more serious proposition is the illegal border trade of arms and drugs- the curse to the local youth.

Table 12.6
Employment Elasticity of Different Sectors

	1983-84	1994-00	IX Plan	Future
Agriculture	0.50	0.00	0.50	0.10
Mining	0.69	0.00	0.60	0.00
Manufacturing	0.33	0.26	0.25	0.22
Electricity, Gas & Water supply	0.52	0.00	0.50	0.00
Construction	1.00	1.00	0.60	0.60
Trade	0.63	0.55	0.55	0.50
Trans, Storage & Communication	0.49	0.69	0.55	0.40
Finance	0.92	0.73	0.53	0.50
Community, Social & Personal	0.50	0.07	0.50	0.30
Total	0.41	0.15	0.38	

Source: Planning Commission (2001): Report of Task force on Employment Opportunities

Table 12.6 provides us an insight to the sectors that should be exploited in particular for providing gainful employment opportunities. The present economic model of the country ensures that GDP growth would have a result in larger employment. However, the task force identified the possibilities of job creation in the organized sector even though the share of the organized sector in employment came down from 10% to 7% during the late 80s and, late 90s respectively. Involvement of private corporate sector in agriculture has been the prescription of the task force while the Mckinsey Report for the Government of WB has recommended cultivation of commercial crops instead of foodgrains as the way out for reviving the sagging agricultural sector. The Northeast also needs revival of agriculture. However, with disguised unemployment being a very common feature, employment generation in other sectors becomes necessary.

Literacy

It is high time to recall that the literacy rates in the Northeast are much higher than the national level and therefore the problem of educated unemployment is greater here. Private cost of higher education in Northeast is much less than expected gains from it and possibly unnecessary large number of people pursue higher education. Blaug and others (1969) observes, "...supply has consistently moved ahead of demand so that educated unemployment as a fraction of the stock of educated manpower has remained constant". However, they further observe that the situation is not due to over investment in education but due to market information. The need of the hour is "manpower planning". Human Resource Management can be the ultimate answer to improve functioning of labour markets. And the Northeast has greater potential for utilizing its human resource as a means for economic development.

For the past few years, one of the most successful job creators has been the BPO sector. Business Person Outsourcing has been a great boost to the economy and has been employing over 1 million according to certain estimates. India's advantage in this sector has been, cheap or rather relatively in low priced personals, with English vocabulary skills. It is here that the Northeastern cities can emerge as a trade zone. English being rather popular and often a medium of instruction in school provide a large pool of English speaking youths. Call centres can easily be a profitable business proposition for entrepreneurs of the region. Of course, this sector has great potential for employing a large number of the educated young work force.

Another sector, which can provide immense employment to the educated youth, is education sector itself. Geo-physical conditions provide a pleasant weather in the region for most of the year. Quality schools, residential - some exist in Shillong and its vicinity would be a viable economic proposition. The ever-increasing middle class do not compromise with their children's education. Professionally managed academic institutes, schools in particular could provide jobs to large number of educated youth and residential schools owing to the multiplier effect could play a vital role in the development of the particular region also. The Doon valley's economic prosperity has a lot of contribution from the schools that have been located in the area.

Bezbaruah (2004) pointed out that large out migration of students at the tertiary level from the region to the rest of the county does not speak well of the facilities and quality of higher education in the region. Professional institutes set up the region could well stop the resource flow.

For the educated unemployed, a welcome move should be the introduction of the VAT regime. Such a tax regime would not just boost up government revenue but would be a major employment generator. Accountability of the firm would require better organizational capacity. Maintenance of accounts requires trained personal. Presently traders hardly practice the regulations. Opportunities, particularly for commerce graduates and computer accountants are bound to increase.

Agro-Climatic Condition

The agro-climatic condition in the Northeast suits to the requirement of various horticultural crops. However just cultivation of crops would not be the solution as markets are needed for an effort to thrive. Fruit and vegetable processing has immense potential, and entrepreneurs from the region can easily delve into this sector. Even professionally qualified youths of the region can organize further small-scale industries like meat and poultry products, cereal based products, confectioneries, feed production etc. SSIs have greater employment generally capacity and are generally favoured by the development planners.

The annual survey of industries observes that large corporate sector has employment potential of 3.63 million whereas the small-scale sector has 17.9 million. Fiscal incentives announced have been to an extent, successful in drawing investment in the region. However, the major lacunae of the region have been its poor infrastructure. Transportation within the region itself is cumbersome. Limited railway network delays cargo movement and thereby limits the flow of perishable goods to distant markets. Better infrastructure certainly ensures greater mobility thereby a larger market. Initiatives on road building would certainly boost up the economy in the long run, but in the short run would also generate huge employment for laborers and skilled workers. Another profitable economic option is the construction sector itself. Employment elasticity in this sector is one of the highest. The real estate industry cluster, broadly defined, consists of a collection of industrial and services sector of the economy, such as construction (housing construction, as well as construction of commercial offices, retail and industrial buildings, and infrastructure projects, such as dams, roads and bridges), brokerage services, real estate finance services (mortgage banking, real estate investment), real estate operations, proper management, architecture and design. Naturally the upstream and downstream sectors like cement, power, furniture and appliances industry gains too.

The region's industrial expansion is limited following certain unavoidable bottlenecks as is observed in table –12.1. Therefore, employment via growth model would be successful more if the thrust is on primary and tertiary sectors.

Most of the inhabitants of Northeast India are non-vegetarians and love taking fish as part of their meal. But for most cases fishes cooked in this region have been bred in Andhra Pradesh. Pisciculture is a very profitable employment opportunity as the market for the produce is already available. The region has numerous advantages for developing Pisciculture due to the existence of many rivers, rivulets and lakes around.

The wetlands and rivers where fish breed naturally need attention for improving yield. Youth in Northeast can adopt the mulberry-dike fishpond system. This system helps in producing both fish & silk worms in large quality from the same land. In China, yield from ponds which benefit from agricultural waste feeding and better stock management is reported to increase 5000-10000 kg per ha per year compared to 50- 200 kg ordinarily.

Natural beauty has been the pride of Northeast. Virgin forest and exotic scenery have remained unemployed for long. Tourism is considered to be very promising sector for the region's economy. The employment potential of tourism sector is one of the highest. Eco- tourism can be a source of revenue to the states and a certain bread earner for the people. Tourism sector owing to its numerous linkages-hotels, restaurants, cabs, buses, guides etc. is way out for the educated youth. Added to it are the boost to the local craftsman and artisans following purchase by the tourists.

Section V

"Employment needs to be restored to its place among the top policy concerns of economic management. The macroeconomic framework agreed to between governments and the Breton Woods Institutions need to focus on employment- not just inflation, GDP growth, short and medium term reforms and short-term fiscal and budgetary targets. They need to set employment targets, which are essential to human development and to sustain future growth" (HDR-UNDP 1996) sums up the policy prescriptions no doubt. The role of the government as the benefactor acquires greater importance in the present day context of the Northeast, especially due to large number of educated unemployed.

Therefore, the first initiative to solve the problem of unemployment is good governance. Efforts at the macro level, to improve infrastructure thereby create job should be the priority. The states should take special initiative for alluring investors in this region. Improved law and order is a necessity to ensure investor confidence. FDIs should be welcomed as technological advancement is in most cases a prerogative of the MNCs. Potentialities for power generation (hydro electric-34920MW accounting for 41.5% of all India potential; natural gas - 7500MW for 10 years; coal - 240MW/dav for 100 years)" should be exploited to the core as it is the basis for the expansion of knowledge based industries. Improvement of internet coil connectivity and installation of broad bandwidth along with other communication facilities should be high on the government agenda.

The governments of the north eastern states should collaborate to form a pressure group so that the Government of India speeds up its trade relation with the South East Asian countries as part of its "Look East policy". A large international market in the vicinity would legalize border trade and be an immense push to the local economy. As a strategic base for foreign and domestic investors willing to explore the SEA market, northeast certainly has a distinct advantage.

The diversified tourist attractions, nature's splendour and cultural heritage need widespread publicity. Selling cost is a part of marketing your product in a monopolistic competitive market and the earlier we learn the better. The tourism sector in the country is a competitive one with the traditional tourist places holding their forte. An additional weapon to market northeast as a tourist destination should be- the low airfare in the region. People in the mainland hardly avail air transport and the lure of air travel should be utilized by the tourism sector of the northeastern states.

Table 12.7
Growth rate of Employment

Sectors	1983-94	1994-00
A. Primary (60.4)	1:60	-O.34
1. Agriculture (59.8)	1.51	-0.34
Mining and Quarrying (O.6]	4.16	-2.85
B.Secondary (16.8)	2.9	2.05
3. Manufacturing [12.10]	2.14	2.05
4. Electricity, gas & water supply (0.3)	4.5	-0.88
5. Construction [4.4]	5.32	7.09
C. Tertiary [22.7]	3.53	2.42
6. Trade [9.4]	3.53	5.04
7. Transport, Storage & Communication [3.7]	3.24	6.04
8. Finance [1.3]	7.18	6.20
9. Community, Social & Personal [8.4]	2.90	0.55
TOTAL	2.04	0.98

Note:- Figures in Parentheses indicate Sectoral employment

Apart from the government initiatives, there should be some micro level efforts too from the people of the region. Innovation, Education and Consciousness are the three mantras that can ensure a better citizen. A better citizen always has a better chance of being successful. Vocational trainings, professional course do improve job prospect and youths should not walk away from it in despair. Traditional institutions of the region are much more effective in organizing their respective societies and their involvement in the development work is more productive. Well, good times are round the corner and are evident with the prime minister being a parliamentarian from the region. However, structural change is a slow process and it takes a long time and tremendous effort to bring about such changes. It is a collective duty of all from the region to ensure the development proposals materialize at the earliest.

REFERENCES

Basic Statistics of the Region, 2002, North Eastern Council.

Bezbaruah, M.P., *Development the North Eastern Region*, 2004.

Blaug, M., P.R.G. Layard & M. Woodhall, *The causes of Graduate Unemployment in India*, 1969.

Dainik Sambad, 18 June, 2004.

Goswami, Atul, Assam's Industrial Development, *EPW*, May 23,1981.

Human Development Report, 1996, UNDP.

Mishra, B.P., keynote address at the National Seminar on *Quest for Development in the North-East India*, Tripura University, 2004.

Report of Task force on Employment Opportunities, 2001, Planning Commission.

Sengupta, Keya, *Disparity in Human Development in the states of North-East India: A threat to Development*, 2004.

Sarma, J. N., Problems of Economic Development in Assam, *EPW*, Vol I, No.7, 1966.

www. northeast. nic. in.

13

YOUTH UNREST IN MANIPUR

—Pradip Phanjoubam

The peculiarity of the youth problem in the Northeast will have to be viewed against the total breakdown of the moral legitimacy of the established order. This background in the Manipur context, informs of something very rotten. The government is today in a total fiscal mess, unable to even nay salaries to its employees regularly. The law and order is in everybody's hands. Corruption has become institutionalized, politics has been reduced to a game of engineering defection and floor crossing, the bureaucracy has very much also become a "kleptocracy", merit is no longer the criteria for either government job recruitment or admission to prestigious courses. In short, the establishment is in a total state of discredit. Against Such a background, it is only expected that the threads that bind the social fabric together are weakened. Sometimes some of the threads snap and things spiral out of control. The context of youth unrest in our society today must have to be assessed against this backdrop.

Militant Reaction

Three kinds of reaction from the youth, impressionable as this section of the society is, have been characteristic. One is an attitude of "I'm OK you are not OK". A social mutation in which certain sections of the population assume a moral high ground and set themselves a militant mission to set right the social disorder and to stem the rot in it. Insurgency to a great extent has been such a response. Such reactions also win sympathy, at least initially, of a larger section of the society, as they are seen to be the "mailed fist" with which the society itself delivers its frustrations at the rotten established order.

Surrender

The second kind of reaction is in the nature of surrender. In this, a loss of the sense of purpose in life is pronounced. This state of directionless is compounded by the sudden explosion of the medium of mass communication, especially in the area of the electronic media. Truthful to the logic that drives these mediums - advertisement revenues - almost all of them without exception, flood urban homes with often delusory images of affluence and consumerism. The youth, particularly the urban and semi-urban, idle, lumpenised category, whose numbers are on a rapid increase, are the worst hit. They latch on to the images of comfort and other trappings of the modern consumerist cultures, which are basically meant for the consumption of affluent societies, causing in the process grave inconsistencies between expectations and the ground reality. Illusory and often detrimental ideals also result. The disparity between what is achievable by them and what they had been made to believe is within their reach, continually widens. The resultant sense of being let down often manifests in deviant behaviours such as drugs abuse, alcoholism, promiscuity, juvenile delinquency etc. The one important moderating influence in affluent societies - that of quality literacy - is also missing, making the youth here all the more vulnerable.

Creative Outlet

But there is also a third way youthful energy finds an expression in Manipur. Thankfully, it has led to immense creativity. In this the excess steam built up within the society finds a sublimated outlet in activities such as sports, theatre and cinema, three areas of activities in which Manipur has been consistently putting up sterling performances. The youth here have also created a niche for themselves in many other performing arts.

Deciphering an Anxiety

It is indeed a surprise that the government has not as yet read the message contained in the grudging approval, if not open applause, by the general public at the manner many insurgent groups are launching crusades against some of the most detested social practices in the state, many of which are actually eating into the very vitals of the society itself. Issues, like corruption, cheating in examinations, alcoholism, drug addiction, food adulteration etc., are very much of deep concern of the public, but ones in which they have so far been swept along, helpless as individuals to stand against the waves. No doubt this passivity to deviant social norms betrays a vital weakness in our society, but it is for the government to provide the moral support needed for them to stand up and fight these scourges. Unfortunately, nothing like this has been happening. The vacuum the government leaves thus, are being filled up by the parallel governments, and quite naturally so. It is a very volatile situation for it sows the seed for a complete loss of public faith in the establishment. But the fact is, despite the civil society's general aversion to the violent and even brutal justice seen being meted out, they are caught in a very tricky situation. As vocal members of the civil society, the Press understands this slippery situation only too well. Leave aside the dangers of making open criticisms of the "parallel governments", the question is, with how much justification before the eyes of the general public can anybody oppose a crusade against, say corruption or alcoholism? How effectively can a fight against known social scourges be criticized, even if it is the Devil himself who has taken up the cause?

The fact of the matter again is, regardless of the brutality involved in the kind of "justice" dispensed by the underground organizations, they have succeeded in addressing certain very deep-rooted concerns of our society today. In this matter, the government has only itself to blame for surrendering this vital

Initiative of working in tandem with the pulse that beat in the very heart of our civil society. By its sheer poverty of commitment, sensitivity, idea, vision and above all political will, the government over the years have not been able to find an adequate and legitimate language to address these same concerns of the people. Morally, we cannot think of a bigger failure of governance than this. We also still fail to understand why the government (or rather government after government) has failed to tackle this problem. Why is the state still mired in corruption at every level of the government? Why has our government schools not performed in all these years? Why is the government still so casual about the work culture in its offices? Answering these questions, and many more of similar nature, honestly, would already be a giant step towards a resolution to the problem at hand. But nobody in the government is willing to go through this soul searching? Not many are ready, or are even interested in looking a little beyond the self, never knowing that this is exactly the kind of myopia that will ultimately threaten to sink the enterprise that we know as Manipur, in which all of us, including those given the charge of steering it, stand in together. In this regard, the tough stand of no negotiation with kidnappers taken by the Okram Ibobi government in the most recent and atrocious case of commissioner IS Laishram, is a change from past strategies in meeting such eventualities. But this is hardly enough. The government must first of all discover the critique provided by all the crusades launched by various underground organizations, and then try and answer some of the questions we have posed? Only such an effort will make it capable of finding the language so urgently needed to engage the serious internal discourses in our civil society born out of deeply entrenched anxiety that their world is about to collapse on account of the visible decay of the established order.

Liberation from Poverty

How poor is Manipur? There are a few very rich, belonging to the business class and the top echelon of government services, many, if not most, are wealthier than their known sources of incomes. Then there are about 80,000 in various government services who can be classified as the middle class, and a vast majority who are outside of these two broad categories of occupations, whose economic status or well being have not been properly assessed. Agriculture is the acknowledged mainstay of the state's economy, but this does not necessarily mean our farmers are rich. In fact most of them are marginal or landless farmers subsisting on the practice of sharecropping, whereby they keep a share of the paddy they cultivate for the landowners. A great majority of our farmers are indeed poor peasants, who would, like most others in Manipur, consider it is a boon if their children make into any government service, which are incidentally the only steady, secure jobs in a state languishing in economic doldrums. There is also hardly any industry worth the name in the state, so employment in this sector has to be next to nil. There is, however, a fledgling private sector, consisting mostly of small scale enterprises which sector, consisting mostly of small-scale enterprises which can employ apart from the entrepreneur himself a few more. So by a conservative estimate, the number of people with a respectable income, including the 80,000 or so government employees, cannot be much more than a lakh, and by a liberal estimate, three times that number. What about the rest of the state's 25 lakh population? Are all of them depending on the 1 to 3 lakh people with a "respectable" income? We are inclined to think the problem is much larger than even the awesome picture sketched by the official figure of 4 lakhs unemployed youths registered with the government employment exchange. In the capital Imphal itself, in every leikai there are many families unable to afford two square meals a day. Worse still, the spectre of poverty is growing more and more menacing with each passing year. And when hunger is growing, can anger be receding?

The peace talks in New Delhi, and the agitation for territorial integrity at home are taking up everybody's full attention at this moment. These are very immediate agendas before us, needing to be tackled with the urgency of a firefight, but their long-term solution will have to be in the state's ability to overcome some of the fundamental issues before it, the most important of which is poverty. That is to say, a way must be found to give the state's economy a fresh direction and vim. It must be made to be able to generate income and employment, not artificially as in the government sector all these years, but out of an intrinsic need to have more people contribute to a growing and vibrant economic machine. If our experts are certain opening up the eastern doors to make Manipur an economic thoroughfare between the west and the east is a solution, this must be lobbied for with political intent and conviction. We are now convinced more than ever, there can be no liberation greater than the freedom from the shackles of poverty and utter hopelessness.

Shared Prosperity is All

We do not believe the ethnic question is as simple as to have only an economic interpretation, but economy is definitely a huge factor. A widely shared prosperity amongst different ethnic groups, different states, different districts... living in the same political environment, can mitigate mutual hostilities and mistrusts considerably. This is our conclusion so far from whatever we have been witnessing in Manipur, or for that matter, the entire northeast region.

Many of the causes for the sense of disparity and injustice felt amongst the population in the hill district of Manipur, if we analyse closely, are to a great extent out of the bounds of the state to settle with the resources in its hands at the moment. The state's economy today generates very little income. Its annual entitlements are also barely enough to pay even the salaries of the 80,000 and odd government employees. Salaries being an urgent obligation, the government had been forced to divert all funds for longer term obligations, including development, to this account, with the result that the economy is condemned further and further into stagnation, and we shiver to say it, its deathbed. This is a compulsion any government that comes to power, led by whichever political party, under the chief ministership of a hillman or a plainsman, will be faced with. It is a very dangerous quicksand we are all in, and unless something big happens, we can all very well sink to our doom. The alarming part of it is, at this very moment, there is little hope that the situation will improve. Avenues for fresh income generating activities are still out of sight. There are two ways out, at least logically. One is impractical and the other hypothetical. The first is the romantic option of reverting to living just within our means. The problem is, this means is extremely small and living within it would mean extreme austerity measures, including the abandonment of all trappings of modern living, and accepting a ration regime even on foodstuff. The impracticability of such a reversion is seen in the manner in which even superficial austerity measures such as a ban on recruitment to government jobs, cuts in perks, closing down of loss making and redundant public sector corporations etc, are objected tooth and nail. The second option is more of a wishful thinking. It will involve our economy finding legs fit enough to join the competitive race of rest of the world. This will entail a number of causalities of history, politics, geopolitics, luck and most important of all, the people's own will and industry, intersecting. We are not in a favourable circumstance in all of these factors at the moment, and the key to changing this destiny, will have rest on the last of the factors named. We have now to abandon romantic daydreaming and begin reassessing our common predicament, and in the process develop a vision rooted in reality. Apart from an iron will and endurance, the pursuit of this vision will need a liberal infusion of fuel to kick-start the effort. As for instance, a Rs 1050 crore token of goodwill from some generous soul, not for hiking salaries and benefits, but to chart out an economic roadmap of the state for the future, can do tremendous good.

Mainstream Problem

Another very strong factor behind youth problem in Manipur is the question of identity. To understand this aspect of the problem, it is imperative to discuss the whole concept of the Indian mainstream. For far too often have we heard the political rhetoric of the need for all to join the "mainstream" (we suppose as opposed to a "sub-streams"). The logic seems sound, provided no attempt is made to scrutinize the issue further. The trouble begins when a more precise definition of the understanding "mainstream" is sought. In the Indian context especially, we are still at a loss what exactly should be considered to be the "mainstream". In this incredibly diverse country, there are over 3860 jatis, speaking more than 1,100 distinct linguistic strains, over 350 of which are in the Northeast region alone. At last count, there are 19 officially recognized major Indian languages listed in the 8th Schedule of the Indian constitution, Bodo, being the latest entry. Statistics to prove this fabled Indian diversity will be endless. Thankfully, the founding fathers of this nation were able to not only appreciate the beauty in this diversity, but also acknowledged the need to give the distinctness of each cultural community the space to maintain their perceived sense of uniqueness, and gave the nation and its citizen a secular, (socialist), democratic, republic. By the guarantee of this constitution, every citizen is (or herself), every religious or linguistic community to be itself, until and unless the exercise this freedom interferes with the freedom guaranteed other citizens, or the nation as a whole.

What exactly would be, or should be, the Indian "mainstream" against this background then? Should it remain as a broad understanding, or should attempts be made to define it in definite terms? As for us, we would without hesitation opt for the former for we are definitely of the opinion that India is beautiful precisely because of its diversity and that any attempt to homogenize this kaleidoscope of cultures into a single "mainstream" would be next to criminal. On a smaller canvas, we can say the same of Manipur. As a matter of fact, a lot of the reasons for the Northeast regions' inability to integrate totally with the Indian consciousness, has been because of the attempt in the past to structure the Indian "mainstream" too precisely as a cultural and historical stream originating about 5000 years ago in the Indus Valley and flowing down across the Gangetic plains into the Bay of Bengal. Here too, there are problems now, because geographically must of the Indus Valley today falls in Pakistan, and a good part of the Gangetic plains in Bangladesh. We can, however, sense a loosening up of the definition of the "mainstream" almost concurrently with the liberalization trend of the Indian economy ever since the early 1990s. Except for some die-hard religious zealots, there have been some very successful attempts to broaden the "mainstream" to accommodate the "sub-streams" as they are, without insisting on them to leave their past behind and merge with their new destiny as defined by the "mainstream." The old understanding of the "mainstream" as a homogenizing force, we would even contend, is against the liberal spirit of the Indian constitution.

This is not a suggestion that there should be no binding threads that keep the widely disparate elements of the Indian nation together. The secular, democratic, constitution, with very definite contours but flexible at the same time because it is amendable, is the best instrument for bringing this into effect. It clearly defines who an Indian is, and what it takes to be n Indian in letter and spirit. It is the seminal material as we' as the guideline for all Indian laws. Stick by its ethos, even if it needs to be reshaped in parts, big or small, and what will be achieved is the realization of the secular, democratic dream of constitutional liberalism. Liberalism on its own can, and in fact will descend into anarchy, which is why the need for a non-arbitrary, constitutional liberalism. It is sad that people still talk of "mains treaming" with its clear ring of cultural and religious chauvinism, without even referring to this well conceived secular instrument at hand. In spite of the strong wind of liberalization, what we still have today is the undercurrent of cultural Indian nationalism. And so, even to this day, many are unable to accept Sonia Gandhi as an Indian. Her being rejected as a bad politician is understandable, but not when it is by the colour of her skin. By the same virtue, a greater part of the Northeast region, still remain culturally and spiritually alienated. We fail to understand why this whole concept of unity in diversity is so difficult for people to fathom.

New Epoch, New Issues

Of the many problems that Manipur faces today, one of the most overwhelming is a missing sense of time amongst its people. Its politics, its debates and in fact much of its life are still confined within yesterday's slogans, yesterday's manifestos, yesterday's outlook and yesterday's ego. For some reason or the other, the society seems simply unable to see or interpret its present reality with the idioms and paradigms thrown up by the greatly altered new world order. It seems caught up in a peculiar time warp of its own. This can have tragic consequences even in the not so distant future. The first bitter pill that it has to swallow seems to be an acknowledgement that it no longer lives in a closed world.

The kingdoms and principalities, as well as tribes and communities that were once perceived as powers in this insular universe have now to be placed in a much greater perspective. A new geopolitical situation, in which even the once awesome machines that moved the expansive British Empire have been circumscribed to be not much more than a footnote in the modern scheme of things. Unless it is able to come to terms with this reality, there are little chances for it to escape failure as a people and succeed in joining the mainstream of the new world.

As of now, luck is not on its side. Its location on the globe, seen in conjunction with the turn of modern history is nothing enviable. Not just Manipur, but the entire northeast India and northwest Myanmar, have little significance on this new geopolitical map, and this is a reality. One example will illustrate. In the information age that the 21st Century is described as, it is hard to sell Manipur and the northeast to the rest of the world. Why the rest of the world, it is difficult to sell the region even to the rest of India. There have been much talks about the national and international media literally blanking out news of the northeast, but what the place have to also realize is the implicit message in the phenomenon is the fact that there are little or no buyers of the northeast.

At the moment, the brightest hope for a shift in the present geopolitics to lift the northeast out of the current blind spot of the world is a political and economic ferment in neighbouring Myanmar. Our location then, as a bridgehead between the huge South Asian market and the South East Asian market, will give it back its significance. The mess that the region is in, with myriad insurrections pulling in different directions, and a politics that has failed abjectly to be in the driver's seat, is only hastening our own decay with every ticking second. The new epoch needs new issues. The northeast must live up to this expectation and prepare to discard yesterday's slogans and set new political and economic agendas in tune with the modern.

APPENDIX

Some Parameters of development in the Northeast

States/ Parameters	Arunachal Pradesh	Assam	Manipur	Meghalaya	Mizoram	Nagaland	Tripura	NEI
Area (Sq.km)	83743	78523	22327	22429	21087	16579	10492	255180
Forest (%)	63	27.41	78.64	42.33	75.11	21.60	57.77	49.7
Population (2001)	1091117	26638407	2388634	2306069	891058	1988636	3191168	384950
Sex Ratio	901	932	978	975	938	909	950	937
Density	13	340	107	103	42	120	304	150.85
Literacy (%)	54.74	64.28	68.87	63.31	88.49	67.11	73.66	65.72
Male Lit. (%)	64.07	71.93	77.87	66.14	90.69	71.77	81.47	72.93
Female Lit. (%)	44.24	56.03	59.60	60.41	86.13	61.92	65.41	57.95
NSDP (current) Rs. Lakh	134852	2505096	255430	280620	135892	–	364557	–
Per capita (current) Rs.	14781	9612	11370	11678	12535	–	9768	–
Airports	0	6	1	1	1	1	1	11
Rail –km	1.26	2373.5	1.35	0	1.5	12.85	44.72	2435.1
National Highway	270.68	2338	434	466.34	430	365.38	333	4637.4

(Contd...)

States/ Parameters	Arunachal Pradesh	Assam	Manipur	Meghalaya	Mizoram	Nagaland	Tripura	NEI
State Highway	0	2144	1437	990.84	261.5	1094.6	454	6381.9
Power Gen. (MW)	66.89	867	7.4	-	18.45	10	312.3	1282.0
Post office (Nos.)	294	3875	682	488	390	307	712	6748
Banks (Branches)	99	1281	104	212	90	94	218	2098
University	1	5	2	1	1	1	1	12
Colleges (degree)	7	226	29	45	29	40	14	390
Schools	1821	44979	2788	6301	2414	2057	5623	65983
Technical Institutes	4	51	9	8	2	7	7	88

2 The Strength of Northeast

- vast power potential through use of hydroelectric energy, natural gas and coal
- rich mineral resources like-limestone, dolomite, granite, sillimanite, quartzite, feldspar
- abundant forest resources
- cheap and easy labour availability
- proximity to South East Asia
- considerable population with English speaking skills -tourist attraction

BIBLIOGRAPHY

Agarwal, Anil (1982): *1000 Crime Quiz*, Rupa & Co.

Agarwal, B.B., Sethi and Gupta (1976): Physical and Cognitive effects of chronic bhang (Canabis) intake, *Indian Journal of Psychiatry*, 1(1).

Ahluwalia, B.K., *Social Change in Manipur*, Delhi, 1984.

Ahuja, Ram (1978): College youth and drug abuse: A sociology study of nature and incidences of drug abuse among the college students in Jaipur (mimeograph), Deptt. of Sociology, Rajasthan University, Jaipur.

Ajwani, J.K. (1985): Some psychological correlates of drug dependence, *Indian Journal of Psychiatry*, 12: 23.

Basic Statistics of the Region, 2002, North Eastern Council.

Berer, Marge, Safe Sex, Women's Reproductive Rights and the Need for a Feminist Movement in the 21st Century, *Reproductive Health, Maters*, Vol.8, No 15, May 2000.

Beyrer, Chris, Salam Irene-Interventions by women for women drug users – Makhais Seminar – Ref - *A Brief Historical Overview-*

Bezbaruah, M.P., *Development the north Eastern Region*, 2004.

Bimola, Ksh, Manipur Women-a study; In Sanajaoba Singh (Ed.), Manipur Past and Present (The Heritage and ordeals of a Civilization), New Delhi., Vol. I, 1988.

Blaug, M., P.R.G. Layard & M. Woodhall, *The causes of Graduate Unemployment in India*, 1969.

Chaki Sirkar, Manjushri, *Feminism in a Traditional Society: Women of the Manipur Valley*, New Delhi, 1984.

Chitnis, S. (1974): *Drug on the College Campus*, Tata Institute of Social Science, Bombay.

Cuddington, John (1993), "Modeling the Macroeconomic Effects of AIDS, with an Application to Tanzania.

Cuddington, John (1993), Further results on the Macroeconomic Effects of AIDS, The Dualistic, Labour – Surplus Economy.

Das and Purkayastha (eds), *Border trade: North-East India and Neighbouring Countries*, Akansha Publishing house, New Delhi.

Desai, Neera and M. Krishnaraj, *Women and Society in India*, New Delhi, 1987.

Desai, Vasant, *Entrepreneurship and Small Bussiness Management*, Himalaya Publishing House, Mumbai, 2000.

Dreze and Sen, *India: Economic Development and Social Opportunity*, Oxford University Press, 1995.

Drug Abuse in India (1977): Report of the Committee appointed by the Government of India, Ministry of Health and Social Welfare, New Delhi.

Drug Situation and Demand Reduction Activities in Thailand, National Council on social Welfare, Thailand, 1994.

Drug Use and HIV Vulnerability-Task Force on Drug Use and HIV Vulnerability.

Epidemiological Analysis of HIV/AIDS in Manipur up to August 2006.

Fifteenth International Day Against Drug Abuse and illicit Trafficking, Joint publication, United Nations Drug Control Programme, Manipur State AIDS Control Society, Social Welfare Department, Manipur and NGOs).

Global Illicit Drug Trends – 2002, ODCCP Studies on Drugs and Crime, UN Office for Drug Control and Crime Prevention.

Goddwin, D.W., (1981): *Alcoholism*, Oxford University Press.

Goswami, Atul, Assam's Industrial Development, *EPW*, May 23, 1981.

Hajarimayum, Jubita, "*Meitei women in Transition in Manipur*, 1997, unpublished M. Phil dissertation, Centre for social medicine and community health, JNU, New Delhi.

Hangzo C, Chatterjee A, Sarkar S et al. 1997, *Preaching out beyond the hills: HIV prevention among injecting Drug Users in Manipur*, India.

Hirashima, Social Sector of Economic Development: A Japanese Perspective, *Indian Social Science Review*, Vol. 4, No. 1, Jan-June, 2002.

International Conference on Drug Abuse and Illicit Trafficking, Vienna, 17-26 June, 1987.

International Narcotics Control Strategy Report-2002, Bureau for International Narcotics and Law enforcement affairs, US states.

Journal of the North Eastern Council, North-Eastern Council, Shillong.

Kalra, R.M., (1955): *Drug Addiction in Schools*, Sterling Publishers, New Delhi.

Kangleipak Business Review, Department of Commerce, Manipur University, Imphal.

Kauti, Defo. B., Effect of socio-economic disadvantages and Women's Status on Women's Health in Cameroon, *Social science and Medicine,* Vol. 4, No.7, 1997.

Khamka, S.S., *Entrepreneurial Development*, S. Chand & Co., New Delhi, 2002.

Mali, D.D., *Entrepreneurship Development in North East*, Indian Institute of Entrepreneurship, Guwahati, 2000.

Ministry of Health & Health Welfare (1976), *Drug Abuse in India: Report of an Expert Committee*, New Delhi.

Mishra, B.P., Keynote address at the National Seminar on *Quest for development in the North-east India*, Tripura university, 2004.

People's Power Against Drug addictive changes in South East Asia, *Harvard Asia Quarterly*, September 2002.

Pinto, Anna, Jubita, Hajarimayum, Community Response to Violence Against women in Manipur, Paper presented at *IXth National Women's Conference on Women's Studies*, Hyderabad, 2000.

Pisani, Elizabeth, AIDS into 21st Century: Some Critical Considerations, *Reproductive Health Matters*, Vol.8, No 15, May 2000.

Political Declaration and Global Programme of Action, UN Decade Against Drug abuse, 1991-2000.

Prasain, G.P., *Entrepreneurship Development*, Sunnmarg Publishers and Distributors, New Delhi, 2003.

Puri and Mishra, *Indian economy*, Himalaya Publishing House, New Delhi, 2002.

Rao, J.V. Prabhakara, *Entrepreneurship and Economic Development*, Kanishka Publishers and Distributors, New Delhi, 2000.

Rapid Situation Assessment, 2000-UNESCO/Kripa Society.

Report of Task Force on employment Opportunities, 2001, Planning Commission.

Revisiting the hidden epidemic – a situation assessment of drug use in Asia in the context of HIV/AIDS: India case, Centre for Harm Reduction, Australia, Jan. 2002.

Salm, Aagje Papineau, promoting Reproductive and Sexual Health in the Era of Sector-Wide Approaches (SWAPs), *Reproductive Health Matters*, Vol. 8, No 15, May 2000.

Sanamani, Yamben " Nipilan: Manipur women's Agitation 1939", *Economic and Political Weekly*, Vol X, No. 8, 1976.

Sarma, J.N., Problems of Economic development in Assam, *EPW*, Vol I, No.7, 1966.

Sengupta, Keya, *Disparity in Human Development in the states of North-East India: A threat to Development*, 2004.

Singh, A.D., (1992)" Survey of Drug abuse in Manipur", Indian Medical Association Manipur State Branch.

Singh, B., (2001), Drug Abuse and AIDS Menace, J.C. Thomas & Others (2001), *Manipur: Constraints in Development of Manipur*, Regency Publications, New Delhi.

Statistical Hand Book of Manipur, Directorate of Economics and Statistics, Government of Manipur, 2001.

Status Report Manipur (2004-205), Manipur state AIDS Control Society, Imphal, Manipur.

Sudhir, H. and Hajarimayum Jubita (Eds), *Violence Against Women in North East India*, Akansha Publishing House, New Delhi, 2005.

Tarapot, *Drug Abuse and Illicit Trafficking in North Eastern India*, Vikas Publishing House, New Delhi, 1997.

Women and Substance Abuse, Elizabeth Ettore, Prof. of Sociology, University of Plymouth, U.K.

World Drug Report 2000, UN Office for Drug Control and Crime Prevention, Oxford University Press, 2000.

Yojana, Ministry of Information and Broadcasting, Government of India, New Delhi.

INDEX

A

Abuse pattern, 57
Adolescent girls, 47
Adolescents boys, 44
Ahanthem, Chitra, 50
Alcohol, 57
All India Employment Exchanges Statistics, 89
Amphetamine type stimulants (ATS), 83, 84
Annual survey of industries, 123
Anti-cease fire extension, 25
Asian countries, 1
Asian countries, 36
Australia, 83
Ayurveda, 34

B

Beginnings, 1
Bhowmick, Indraneel, 111
Brahmaputra, 119
Breton Woods Institutions, 125
Broad objective, 5
Business Person Outsourcing, 121

C

China, 35, 83, 84
Compound annual growth rate (CAGR), 113
Corruption, 112

D

Das, Gurudas, 8
Das, Gurudas, 89
De-addiction, Centre, 17
Deadly drugs or hard drugs, 11
Devi, Romeobala S., 10
Diazepam, 53
Drug abuse amongst youths in Manipur, 50-55
  consequences on health, 50-51
  – – society, 51-52
  economic consequences, 52
  findings of a survey, 52-53
Drug abuse, 5
Drug addiction, 2
Drug use and the need for social advocacy among adolescents, 34-49
Drug-related personal characteristic, 10-19
  common drugs of abuse, 11
  drug problem, 11-12
  main drugs of abuse, 12
    narcotic drugs, 12-13
    non-narcotic drugs of abuse, 13
Drugs from Myanmar, 10

E

Economic opportunities, 116
Economy of the Northeast India, 115
Educated unemployment, 3
Education in India, 117
Education, 5, 15
Employment elasticity, 123
Employment opportunities in north-east India, 111-127
  agriculture, 119
  agro-climatic condition, 123-124
  education, 117-119
  employment elasticity of different sectors, 120
  geographically the Northeast, 120
  geography of NER, 119 121
  growth rate of employment, 126-127
  land utilization, 115
  literacy, 121-123
  progress of agriculture, 114
  unemployment scenario, 116-117
Employment, 91, 116, 125
Entrepreneurship education and training, 98-110
  causes of unemployment, 101
    jobles growth, 101
    increase in labour force, 101-102
    inappropriate technology, 102
  demerits of present education system, 104-105
  employment in organized and unorganized sectors, 100
  entrepreneurship and education, 106-107
  inappropriate education system, 102-103
  introduction, 99-100
  nature of unemployment, 100-101
  unemployment and entrepreneurship, 105-106
  – problems in Manipur, 103-104
Europe, 83

F

Feminine conformity, 46
Fish and silk worms, 124
Friedrich, W. Sertyrner, 77

G

Gender-based violences, 29
Gender perspective, 46
Golden Triangle, 10, 60, 64
Government of India, 118
Gyanendra, 8

H

Hajarimayum, Jubita, 1, 24
Harm reduction, 73
Heroin, 8, 57
Human capital formation, 61
Human Immunodeficiency Virus (HIV)/AIDs, 2, 7, 24, 36, 51, 71
  epidemic in Manipur, 39, 65
  STIs, 26, 31
  transmission, 85
Hyptozen, 53

I

Illegal drug production, 37

Illicit opium-producing, 79
Imphal Municipal Council of Manipur, 20
Imphal Municipal Council, 6
Income, 5
Indo-Myanmar Border, 6, 40
Indraneel Bhowmick, 9
Industrial growth, 115
Injecting Drug Users (IDUs), 6, 7, 20, 26, 37, 38, 40, 51, 58, 72
Injecting of licit/illicit drugs, 42
Introduction, 1-9
Irene, Salam, 6, 34
Issues for development, 56-63
  development issues, 59-62
  drug-abuse in Manipur, 56-58
  indicator of development, 58-59
  introduction, 56

J

Jewelled Land, 98

K

Kabp studies, 20-23
Knowledge Attitude Behaviour Practices, 6

L

Labour, 61
Local clubs, 23
Look East Policy, 125

M

Maharashtra, 58
Mandrax, 53
Manipur, 50-55
Manipur-Myanmar border, 67
Mean age, 57
Meira paibis, 23, 25
Meitei women, 25
Merihuana, 34
Mittal, Anukant, 42
Morphine, 41
Morphine, 8
Myanmar, 83, 85

N

Nature splendor, 126
NDPS Act, 37
NERAMAC, 116
New epoch new issues, 137-138
NGOs, 20, 39
Nisha-Band, 25
Nitrazepam, 53
Nitrosun, 53
Non-economic factors, 116
North America, 83

O

Occupation, 5
Opium and heroin production, 76-88
  Arab traders, 77
  Bayer Pharmaceutical Co., 77
  brief history of opium, 76-80
  chemical structure of opiates, 78
  China, 77
  Chinese ceded Hong Kong to the British Empire, 77
  – term, 81
  drug scenario of Manipur, 85-86
  first opium war, 77
  heroin synthesis, 82
  homers works, 77
  hoppocrates, 77
  morphine extraction from opium, 80-83

– hydrochloride, 81
morphine, 77
odysseys, 77
opium production in
Myanmar, 83-85
raw opium, 80
referral services, 87
second opium war, 77
slaked lime, 80
smoking heroin, heroin
hydrochloride, 83
socio-economic and
demographic profile,
86
abuse of drug abuse,
88
age group, 86
district-wise
distribution, 86
education, 87
family income, 87
marital status, 87
mode of abuse, 87
nature of drug abuse,
88
period of drug abuse,
88
recovery rate, 88
religion, 86
United States Congress,
78
Opium in Myanmar, 40
Opium poppy survey for
Myanmar, 84
Opium, 8
Orpheus, 77

P

Papaver somniferum, 79
Parameters of development,
139
Percentage of abusers, 57
Perennial rivers, 119
Performance of the region, 112
Pethidine, 41
Phanjoubam, Pradip, 128
Poorer women exposure, 28
Poverty, 112
Practices of injecting drugs,
22
Prasain, G. P., 8, 98
Precis of the Canvas, 5
Pre-martial sex, 43
Prodrom, 53

R

Relationship of Education
with drug related personal
characteristics, 15-16
relationship of income
level, 16-17
suggestions, 17
curative aspect, 17-18
preventive aspect, 18-19
Relipin, 53
Reorientation of education,
107-109
Romeobala , 5

S

Sectoral composition of the
NE states, 113
Sero-surveillance, 67
Services sector, 115
Sexual violences, 29
Sexually Transmitted
Infections (STIs), 24
Singh, Gyanendra K., 89
Singh, Ingocha K., 20
Singh, Kumar Bijoy E., 56
Situation in North-east, 112
Social issue, 3
Soft and hard drugs, 5
Southeast Asia, 79
Soviet invasion of
Afghanistan, 36

State security agencies, 29
Sub-Saharan Africa, 65
Substitution drugs, 45
Sudhir, H., 1, 64
Suresh, L., 8, 76

T

Tamil Nadu, 58
Taskforce on Employment Opportunities, 119
Thailand, 83, 84
Tourist attractions, 126
Tripura Jute Mill, 116
Tripura, 116

U

UN Human Development Reports, 65
Unemployed registered, 118
Unemployment in Manipur, 89-97
 exchange, 91
 primary sector, 94
 secondary sector, 95
 tertiary sector, 95
Unemployment, 3, 4, 109, 112

V

Vallium, 53

W

Why do young people take to drugs, 53
Women, 24-33
 gender inequality, 27-29
 – based violence, 29-30
 health facility and education, 30-31
 lower socio-economic status, 26-27
 reproductive health, 27-29
 sexual health, 27-29
 methods of the study, 25-26
 unprotected sex, 28
Women self-esteem, 28
Women's health status, 6
World War II, 36

Y

Youth counselling, 2
Youth unrest in Manipur, 128-138
 creative outlet, 129-130
 deciphering an anxiety, 130-131
 liberation from poverty, 132-133
 mainstream problem, 135-137
 militant reaction, 128-129
 shared prosperity is all, 133-135
 surrender, 129
Youth, drug and development, 64-75
 conceptual setting, 65
 connectivity, 71-73
 picture, 66-69
 problem, 65-66
 responses, 73
 transmission factors, 70-71
Youth's addictive behaviour, 1

Z

Zambia, 58
Zolam, 53

■■■